# The Wider Ecumenism

# The Wider Ecumenism

*by* EUGENE HILLMAN, C.S.Sp.

*Foreword by* PIET FRANSEN, S.J.

HERDER AND HERDER

1968

HERDER AND HERDER NEW YORK

232 Madison Avenue, New York 10016

*Nihil obstat:* G. Feeley

*Imprimatur:* ✠ Dennis Durning, Bishop of Arusha, 27 Jan. 1968

Printed in Great Britain

Set in Linotype Pilgrim

# Contents

5

# Contents

# Foreword

At the opening of the second session of Vatican II, on 29 September 1963, Pope Paul VI condensed in a single question the enormous task of the Council: "Church, what do you say about yourself?" After the revealing discussions on the liturgy and the Church during the first session under John XXIII, this question had indeed become the most urgent challenge facing the gathered leaders of the Roman Catholic Church.

Such a question was not inspired by a kind of introvert apprehension, a sort of egocentric concern for the Church's own perfection and well-being. Quite the contrary. It was Pope John himself who, from the very beginning of the Council, in his opening address on 11 October 1962, unhesitatingly invited the bishops to look outside: to consider above all else how God's providence was confronting the Church of Rome with the Christian world of our separated brothers; and, still further, with the peoples all over the world who also believe in God.

Doubtless this opening up of the Church towards a fraternal dialogue with all men would have remained merely in the realm of ideas, almost as an ephemeral and short-lived dream, were it not for the presence at the Council of so many bishops and theologians from all parts of the world. Never before had there been so wide a participation in an ecclesiastical council; and this presence, representing the "tribes and tongues and peoples and nations", was a refreshing surprise to very many in Rome. At the First Vatican Council there were, of course, a few bishops from the Americas, and fewer still from the non-Western world. But they were, for the most part, European in background

7

and in outlook; so, even aside from their small numbers their influence was not especially notable, nor was their significance manifestly universal.

The Second Vatican Council was something very different. Every theologian in Rome during the first session was struck with the force and the newness of this experience. Especially during the discussions on the liturgy, after an initial period of bewilderment and self-consciousness due to the solemnity of the surroundings and the lack of adequate preparation, one bishop after another from Africa and from Asia stood up to witness, with ever-increasing courage and urgency, to the needs and the hopes of the young Churches. A new vitality and a wider vision were dramatically signified in these events.

What happened at the Council continues to happen today. Catholic theology is confronted with an immense task : to implement the decisions of the Council through a renewal of theological reflection, a reform of the pastoral ministry and of the missionary approach, a sincere re-adjustment of ecclesiastical law and an authentic adaptation of the sacramental dispensation in the liturgy. But this cannot be done alone by theologians in Europe and the Americas. It cannot be done at all without the active participation of theologians in all parts of the world. For it is a catholic undertaking, and must therefore reflect the myriad viewpoints and the diverse problems arising from the living experience of the Church among the nations.

Too often the faith is regarded merely as a private and personal possession; but it is also a corporate "communion", a *koinonia* in faith and love. God speaks to us in history, not only in the depths of one's conscience but also through the many voices of our brothers in the faith. For the re-thinking of our modern existential situation as Christians, wherever we ourselves may be, we need the witness of faith given by our brothers everywhere. This world-wide dialogue and communion in the same faith is most urgently required at the present time. Without such a catholic testimony, it is impossible for us to see the different aspects of the very same problems for which we ourselves, as well as those in other places, are seeking solutions. For the deepest meaning of our faith is found in the Christian's confrontation with the different experiences and the real needs of humanity, including the grim realities of hunger and destitution among our fellow men elsewhere in the world. Their human forebodings and expectations are, just beneath the cultural surface and aside from the historical conditioning, exactly the same as our own.

This exchange of viewpoints in a dialogue of faith calls urgently for the active collaboration of the bishops, priests, religious, and laymen who serve the young Churches of Asia and Africa. Overwhelmed as they are by the pastoral care of the Churches, and suffering from an acute lack of personnel for the normal ministry, this dialogue must nevertheless be accepted by them as an essential part of their burden. It is indispensable for the growth of their catholic vision, as well as for ours. So we in the Western world should be immensely grateful whenever one of them accepts his responsibility to enter into this dialogue, and thus gives his witness to the hopes and experiences of the peoples among whom he serves. The notable contribution offered by Father Hillman in the following pages deserves the gratitude of theologians everywhere. This is the work not only of a well-informed theologian but of one who speaks to us with an uncommon clarity and a prophetical tone.

Having lived in Africa for almost a year myself, while serving on the staff of a diocesan seminary, I have some first-hand understanding of the problems there. I am especially aware of the great difficulties met by anyone who tries to articulate his theological reflections in relation also to what is happening in the theological realms of Europe and the Americas. He suffers from a lack of reference books and library facilities, a scarcity of learned journals and reviews, as also from the pressures of the ministry and a chronic lack of time. But there can be no vital dialogue without an intimate acquaintance with the thoughts and ideas of others. Father Hillman has somehow managed to surmount these formidable difficulties. I particularly admire his grasp of so many aspects of the problems faced by contemporary theology, especially in relation to the delicate and complex matters with which his book is concerned.

The problem of the nature and the meaning of the Church in our time is intimately related to countless other aspects of our faith. It concerns, among other things, the nature of grace and of faith, the meaning of the sacramental dispensation in the Church, and most of all the deep mystery of God's ways with men: "for God is greater than our hearts, and he knows all things" (I John 3:20). But Christians everywhere, from their own living experience among the nations, must try to say to each other what they can about the Church. Otherwise, since the Church is the gathering of all the faithful, there can be no full answer to the question: "Church, what do you say about yourself?"

So it is that the following missionary reflections, on anonymous Christianity and the Church, contain something of value for all of us. The author's message, like that of all authentic Christian theology, emerges from a background of living faith and human experience. This background is "something which has existed from the beginning, that we have heard, and we have seen with our own eyes; that we have watched and touched with our own hands: the Word who is life—this is our subject. That life was made visible:

we say it and we give our testimony, telling you of the eternal life, which was with the Father and has been made visible to us, as we are in union with the Father and his Son Jesus Christ. We are writing this to you, to make our own joy complete" (I John 1 : 1-4).

PIET FRANSEN, S.J.

Innsbruck

# Preface

"To do something for the sake of the Church of the future", Dietrich Bonhoeffer had intended to produce a slim volume dealing with certain things "which we so often prefer to forget". The tragic events of his particular time and place in history prevented his filling out the "very crude and sketchy" outline of his proposed book which was to have only "three chapters and not more than one hundred pages". (Cf. Bonhoeffer's *Letters and Papers from Prison*.)

Others, in countless pages and chapters and volumes, have since dealt with the first and second of these chapter themes. Some of them have done this in ways which Bonhoeffer, were he alive today, would hardly recognize as developments of his original insights, and as answers to his provocative questions: "Humanity comes of age in a time of no religion at all. . . . Is there a religionless Christianity? . . . What *is* Christ for us today? . . . 'God' as a working hypothesis, as a stop-gap for our embarrassments, now superfluous. . . . What do we mean by 'God'?"

But much less has been written on the third chapter theme left by this "prophet of the new era for mankind", although these notes, written by him in prison, contain *his* conclusions to the preceding thoughts. It is not surprising that such conclusions should have been generally overlooked by the sophisticated composers of what has been called "pop" theology: a kind of trafficking in neat phrases and scintillating concepts, which do not really demand the type of traditional Christian commitment that cost Bonhoeffer his life. His conclusions clearly presuppose two realities which are not very novel: a living God and an existing Church. The final theme of Bonhoeffer's outline is this—and it may be taken as a summary of the reflections presented in the following pages: "The Church is her true self only when she exists for humanity."

But my slim volume is no imaginative effort to say what Bonhoeffer might have said on this subject. There are bound to be many variations on the one theme. Each of us sees things only from his own historically conditioned viewpoint. The here and now situation determines our differences of perspective, our shifts in emphasis, in accentuation and in stress. No man has the total view. Does not Bonhoeffer himself, like so many articulate thinkers who have lived only within the frontiers of the Western world, sometimes seem to identify humanity exclusively with *homo occidentalis mechanicus*—forgetting almost that most of mankind really exists in other times and in different places?

Some of the best Christian scholars of our time have already treated the great questions of ecumenism and the mission of the Church in the modern world; and they continue to do so impressively. But they are the first to admit that their vision is quite unavoidably shaped by their situation inside the crumbling walls and the tottering citadels of ancient christendom. To one who lives on the outside, their theologizing appears to have a decidedly post-Christian concern; and their Christian dynamics seem to be almost obsessed by the recently invented notion of "re-evangelization".

My viewpoint is not superior to theirs, nor any more comprehensive. It depends very much on theirs, and yet it is rather different: it is pre-Christian. I have spent the past sixteen years of my life among the mostly "pagan" people of the Masai tribe in northern Tanzania. This is the context in which, and the position from which, I am compelled to consider the relevance of the Church for humanity. So I find it hard to believe that "humanity has come of age in a time of no religion at all".

Just whose supposition is it anyway that Western man, in terms of the essential human experience and the common destiny of mankind, is somehow more mature than everyone else? All men on earth today are equally distant from the beginnings of humanity, and equally close to the end of history. The vast majority of our contemporaries throughout the world are probably still quite as seriously concerned as they have ever been with religion. If nothing more therefore this book may serve as a reminder that most of the world is still waiting for the advent of the Messiah, and that the future of the Church ought not to be conceived in mainly post-Christian terms. At least it will show that there are today, as there have been since the day that Paul withstood Cephas to his face (Gal. 2:11), some theologians with a magnificently catholic vision, transcending the Western ethnocentrism and leaving behind the exclusively ecclesiocentric approach—both of which have characterized so much of what passes for Christian thought.

The future of Christianity does not hinge on the visible re-conversion of the "de-Christianized masses" in parts of Europe and the Americas, nor on the theological interpretation of "the pill". No doubt, these are highly important questions on the provincial level. But a Church, aspiring by her very nature to become universal, might be expected to show a proportionate amount of interest in the far wider questions concerning the significance of God's people in relation to the *oikumene*.

The Church becomes herself only by moving forward in an historical process which is eschatological and therefore unrepeatable. Her future is among the peoples who have not yet known Christ in this sacramental sign of salvation raised up among them—among one new people after another. Is this not one of the things "which we so often prefer to forget"? Hence my effort here, offered tentatively but hopefully, although perhaps a bit too presumptuously, "to do something for the sake of the Church of the future".

My first four chapters are an attempt to state, as clearly and as forcefully as my circumstances permit, this question: Why should the Church exist visibly among any people at any time? Current salvation theology has made this an acutely disturbing question. And, if the widening ecumenical dialogue among religions is going to lead to something more than mutual tolerance, then a convincing answer must be found. We will get nowhere today by just repeating exactly what was said the last time this matter came up for discussion. The elements of a fresh answer are hopefully contained in the subsequent chapters.

As I am more of a practical missionary than a professional scholar, some of the articulations of my viewpoint may sound too clumsy, or too hypothetical; and some readers may even regard them as not "safe" enough. But I am confident that what I am trying to say will, in spite of such reservations, come through to those for whom this book is intended: those who are concerned more with the whole than with the part, and more with the future than with the past.

EUGENE HILLMAN, C.S.SP.

Catholic Mission
P.O. Monduli
Tanzania

# Part One

## THE IMPLICATIONS OF ANONYMOUS CHRISTIANITY

# I

# The Missionary Question

> If it is true in the green wood, what
> hope is there for the others, who have
> sinned like Israel, and still sin, but
> have no part in Israel's distinction, in
> the great measure of grace that it
> received? What hope is there for the
> multitude of the Gentiles in whose
> midst Israel was only an inconsiderable
> minority?
>
> KARL BARTH

A growing awareness of the *universal* reality of salvation is an outstanding characteristic of current theology. This is clearly reflected in the teaching of Vatican II. "Many elements of sanctification and of truth are found outside the visible structure" of the Church; so the "helps necessary for salvation" are always and everywhere available to all who are obedient to "the dictates of conscience".[1] This kind of thinking is optimistic, and it yields a lively tendency to broaden the scope of modern Christian ecumenism.[2]

---

[1] *Dogmatic Constitution*: *Lumen Gentium*, Vatican, 1964, nos. 8, 16.

[2] Cf. Dom Sylvester Houédard, o.s.b., "The Wider Ecumenism", in *The Aylesford Review*, vol. VII, no. 2 (Summer 1965); Dom Odo Brooke, o.s.b., "Natural Religion and the Supernatural Existential", in *The Downside Review*, vol. 83, no. 272 (July 1965); Eugene Hillman, c.s.sp., "Ecumenism and Grace", in *African Ecclesiastical Review*, vol. VIII no. 1 (January 1966), and "'Anonymous Christianity' and the Missions", in *The Downside Review*, vol. 85, no. 277 (October 1966); Frederick J. Streng, "Is there a Gospel in Non-Christian Religions?", in *Dialog*, vol. 6, no. 2 (Spring 1967).

In its original New Testament sense the word *oikumene* is never restricted to the existing communities of Christian belief; it always means the whole inhabited earth to which the new people of God are sent, and from which they are called.[3] Ecumenism and the missionary spirit are finding one another in the realization that Christian faith is given to some men for the sake of all men. The Church exists for the sake of redeemed humanity. So the people of God have meaning only in relation to everyman. Thus the Church, by reason of her catholic aspirations and her present self-examination, is being ever more consciously confronted with whole worlds of religious experience outside the Judeo-Greco-European encounter between God and man in explicit Christian faith. And the Church today is looking upon all these others with a sympathetic understanding which she has not always shown for them in the past.

Some Christians still feel uneasy about all of this. But is not the Christian covenant something absolutely decisive for all men, something that was made from the beginning with everyman? There are so many new questions to be answered these days, questions which have perhaps never before been asked.

If each man, regardless of his own particular time and place in history, is equally distant from God, is not each one objectively in the same condition before God who loves all with the same redeeming love? Who is to decide, and by what criterion, that some of the earth's inhabitants—who happen to live here or there, now and then—are more beloved of God than all the others?

Missionaries, surrounded as they are by non-Christians, are perhaps more acutely sensitive than other Christians to this present problematical condition of the Church in re-

[3] Cf. *The Household of God* by Lesslie Newbigin (SCM Press, London, 1964), p. 18.

lation to the *oikumene*. This is so especially with those missionaries who have seen how really hard it is—indeed, how impossible—to reach most men (the rapidly increasing majority of contemporary mankind) with the saving message of Christianity. The vast inadequacies of the Church are most exposed in "mission lands". New patches on thread-bare garments will no longer suffice. Missionaries cannot afford to wait any longer for professional scholars to answer all of their questions and to provide them with all of the new theological perspectives demanded by the present moment. They must themselves try to re-define their own inner attitudes—and now. For it is now that they are living among non-Christians, and working for them in the name of Christ. How right Karl Barth was when he said that those engaged in the active ministry may not abandon theology to others!

Now what about the overwhelming majority of humanity who, for so many good and bad reasons, are not touched explicitly by the good news of Christian revelation? Is sal·vation for them merely some vague, dubious and extraordin-ary possibility: something *more difficult* and *less assured* for them than for the relatively small segment of men who have been called to historically actual membership in the Church during the past nineteen hundred years? The im-plications of this question are far-reaching. The answer we give will determine, in the most basic way, our future mis-sionary approaches to non-Christian peoples; and it will profoundly shape our attitudes and our manner of partici-pating in any dialogue with the members of other religions. What answers do we have?

Modern theologians assure us that the general condition of non-Christians is "not desperate", because Christ has died that *all* men might attain to everlasting life through his superabounding grace which is, therefore, in God's mysterious ways offered even to those who live visibly outside of the Church. In spite of some dire comments by St Paul on the status of the non-evangelized peoples, even he insists on the revolutionary notion that, in terms of salvation, what is true of Christians must also be true of all men (Rom. 5: 12-21).

In contrast to the pessimistic view expressed in the letter to the Ephesians (2:12; 4:17-19), Paul's underlying affirmations, in harmony with a recurring biblical universalism, suggest "no partiality" (Rom. 2:6, 10-16; 10:20; Col. 1:16, 20, 27; I Tim. 2:4-6; Heb. 2:9-11; 9:26-28).

*"But"*, our most eminent theologians invariably add, the situation of non-Christians is nevertheless "precarious and *obviously less favourable* to salvation than an explicit faith in Christ and visible membership in the Church. . . ."[4] So it is "urgent to put at the disposal of the pagan, who is *normally* as weak and *even weaker* than the Christian, those same means of salvation which will make his task *infinitely easier*, his path *infinitely more secure*, his future *infinitely more favourable*. . . ."[5] For, "it seems that the will of God is really to give the goodwill of men a normal and *easier way* of coming to him, through Christ and the Church."[6]

A more sophisticated variation on this same theme is expressed by Bernard Cooke in an overly psychologized theological reflection on the present relevance of Christianity. "In all parts of the world today," according to this well-known theologian, "religion is faced with the charge of irrelevance and Christianity is not exempt from this

[4] Paul de Surgy, *The Mystery of Salvation* (Sheed & Ward, London, 1966), p. 199, italics added.
[5] Joseph Masson, S.J., quoted in "The Reasons for Missionary Activity" by Domenico Grasso, S.J., in *Teaching All Nations*, vol. 3, no. 2 (October 1966), p. 268, italics added.
[6] Joseph Masson, S.J., *Christian Revelation and World Religions*, Ed. Joseph Neuner, S.J. (Burns & Oates, London, 1967), p. 133, italics added.

charge." Professor Cooke's thoughtful reply to this charge is highly coloured by his own existential situation; and it is based on an inadequately qualified assertion that Christianity's patterns of thinking, patterns of basic attitude, and patterns of behaviour make it possible for man to be "more profoundly human". Non-Christians might ask : "More profoundly human than whom exactly?" "And where is the existentially pertinent evidence for such an assertion today?" But the point of interest here is the precise reason given for the relevance of the Christian religion : it provides "meaning" and "understanding" and "psychological security" for those who are in need of self-identification, authentic community experience, self-location in intelligible patterns of historical understanding, a sense of achievement and purpose in a sea of human anonymity, etc., within those "evolutionary dimensions of reality" which university professors find so intriguing.

This answer is, however, not nearly as wide as the question it is supposed to be dealing with, concerning the universal relevance of Christianity for all men "in all parts of the world". It is no answer at all for those countless millions of men in the non-Western world, who do exist with meaning for themselves and their brothers in vital human communities (which are sometimes called "underdeveloped"); who do have a sense of achievement and purpose within their respective cultural horizons (which are not necessarily more limited than the horizons of Chicago's population); who are truly open to other men in a relatively wide range of personally creative experiences; who do find sufficient "psychological security" in their own traditional religions; and who are *also* tempted to regard themselves as "more profoundly human" than the rest of men. In other words, what we need is a *universally pertinent* answer to the question of Christianity's relevance for men in all times

23

and places: not merely in the context of modern Western man's problem of "psychological security".[7]

The common view among conservative Protestant theologians, according to one of them,[8] is that, while Christ died for all men, "the benefits of His atoning sacrifice, the pardon from God that includes the forgiveness of sins, cannot be said to exist either juridically in the mind of God or experientially in the hearts of men, *until* they have been faced with the free invitation of the Gospel and have either embraced it or rejected it." This explicit "Gospel repentance" is thus the necessary means by which "men avail themselves of what is *only potentially* theirs and which, in fact, becomes theirs only when they repent. . . ." The same theologian continues: "This means and can only mean that men have not yet been reconciled to God by Christ; that they have, by His death and Resurrection, been placed in a position where they *can be* reconciled. But whether they benefit from what Christ died to give them will be determined by their repentance towards God and faith towards the Lord Jesus Christ. . . . There is no hope for the present world as we know it, but the Christian looks for a recreated world with a new heaven and a new earth, where righteousness dwells. . . ." From this theological position it follows, with a tacit assumption about the hopeless (or at least very precarious) condition of those who have not yet been "faced with the free invitation of the Gospel", that "the mission of the Church, first and foremost, is proclamation for the salvation of men. . . ."

There are some weighty and long-standing arguments in support of the theological vision presented by the Catho-

[7] "Existential Pertinence of Religion", in *Concilium*, vol. 9, 2 (1966), pp. 17 ff.; in the American edition of *Concilium*: vol. 19, pp. 32 ff.

[8] Harold Lindsell, "A Rejoinder", in *International Review of Missions*, vol. LIV, no. 216 (October 1965), pp. 437 ff., italics added in the following quotations from this article.

lic and Protestant theologians just cited. But is it really so "obviously" the way things are : that non-Christians are in such a "less favourable" position? Is there no room here for further inquiry? Perhaps it is possible to give a rather different theological interpretation of the religious condition in which most men, without any historically conscious reference to Christ but nevertheless within the one merciful dispensation of divine providence, are expected to pursue their common human destiny in relation to God.

The current Christian awareness of God's unbounded love for men is frequently articulated, particularly in the writings of Karl Rahner and Edward Schillebeeckx, under the heading of "anonymous Christianity". Among Protestant theologians this might be categorized as a kind of qualified universalism. The very many real and imagined implications of this notion have provoked some vigorously negative reactions,[9] and they have contributed notably to the so-called "crisis in the missions".[10] The ordinary missionary in the field tends to state the central question something like this : "If men can be saved without having explicitly encountered the Gospel, and without participating consciously in the life of the Church, then where is the urgency of missionary work?" The same question might be pushed even further—to the perplexity of Christians everywhere: "Why should the Church exist visibly anywhere at any time?"

To question the meaning of missionary activity is at once to question the reasons for the very existence of the Church. The missionary task, according to the specific teaching of Vatican II on this subject, "is the highest and most holy

[9] For example : *The Catholic Encounter with World Religions* by H. van Straelen, s.v.d. (Burns & Oates, London, Newman Press, Westminster, 1966); *What of the Unevangelized?* by J. O. Saunders (Overseas Missionary Fellowship, London, 1966).

[10] Cf. *Christ to the World*, vol. X, no. 4 (1965), pp. 289-99, 347-50, 355-7; and subsequent issues of this review.

function of the Church."[11] If this function is at all dispensable, or even secondary in relation to all of the other problems of the Church today, then just how necessary is the Church for the salvation of the world? If Christians wish to reorient themselves in ways which are more relevant to the world, then they might best start by clarifying for themselves the meaning and the relevance of missionary activity as such.[12] It is only through her "highest and most holy function" that the authentic nature of the Church can be understood.

It is not enough simply to repeat over and over again that, since the Church is missionary by her very nature, her missionary activity is necessary, as it involves the salvation of the world somehow. This is profoundly true. But why? And how is this truth related to the special historical vocation of God's explicit people who are, and must become ever more fully, the universal sacrament and eschatological sign of mankind's salvation? In the answer to this question will be found the keenest incentive for a total renewal of the Church's original Pentecostal élan. In the meantime, what is the usual answer given to the question asked above concerning the urgency of missionary activity?

The immediate reaction to the question is usually this: to admit, sometimes rather reluctantly, that salvation is "possible" for all whose ignorance of the Church is inculpable; and so it is *conceded* that missionary work is not "exclu-

---

[11] *Decree: Ad Gentes*, Vatican, 1965, no. 29; also no. 35, where this work is called "the fundamental duty of the people of God".

[12] *Ibid.*, no. 6: "The proper aim of this missionary activity is to preach the Gospel and plant the Church among the peoples and groups for whom the Church has not yet been established (*in quibus nondum radicata est*)." This "not yet" specifies the matter, so missionary activity is not the proper name of any and every function through which the Church seeks to fulfil her total mission: it is simply *one* of the "varied ministries" (I Cor. 12:4-6) or "different functions" (Rom. 12:4-6) through which the *one mission* of the Church is being achieved progressively.

sively", nor even "primarily", a matter of "saving souls" directly. It is then asserted, often quite emphatically, that this work is nevertheless necessary, because it provides an ever increasing number of men with "more opportunities for grace" and, therefore, with "a better chance of attaining salvation".

The supposition is that salvation is really "easier" or "more assured" or "more available" for the Church's visible members than for all the others who have known Christ only implicitly or anonymously. The assumption is that, while the breathing of the Holy Spirit is not confined within the limits of the visible Church, His breath is somehow more effective when channelled through an external ecclesiastical structure.

Such a reply is obvious, facile and common. It appears, moreover, to have some basis in the writings of Karl Rahner who says that explicit Christian faith and visible membership in the Church "offers a greater chance of salvation for the individual than if he had remained simply an anonymous Christian."[13] The same position is reflected in the popular theology of Charles Davis who wrote that implicit faith among the unevangelized is "a mutilated faith" belonging to "cripples in the life of faith".[14] Certainly this represents a notable improvement over Cardinal Louis Billot's theory which would consign most of humanity to a purely natural end, never mentioned in Scripture, called "Limbo".[15]

[13] Cf. "Christianity and non-Christian Religions" by Karl Rahner, s.j., in *The Church: Readings in Theology*. Compiled at the Canisianum-Innsbruck (P. J. Kenedy & Sons, New York, 1963), p. 133; also "Rahner's 'Anonymous Christian'" by K. Riesenhuber, s.j., in *Theology Digest*, vol. XIII, no. 3 (Autumn 1965), p. 171; but, presumably, Rahner's "individual" has been adequately confronted with the explicit Gospel; see p. 57, below.

[14] Cf. *The Study of Theology* by Charles Davis (Sheed & Ward, London, 1964), p. 133.

[15] Cf. *The Wide World My Parish* by Yves Congar, o.p. (Darton, Longman & Todd, London, 1961), p. 101.

Is it not possible now to take one further step in the same general direction? The theological opinions cited so far in this chapter seem to signify a progressive development from the very same basic insight, that there must be some third way between the two extremes suggested by a too literal interpretation of the Lord's own words on the necessity of baptism for salvation: "Unless a man be born of water and the Holy Spirit, he cannot enter into the kingdom of God" (John 3:5). This is precisely why Peter Abelard, a little more than eight hundred years ago, came out with his original "limbo hypothesis" in the first place. This was a preliminary effort to safeguard the Church's belief in the universality of salvation, against the "zealots of damnation" who saw salvation and damnation exclusively in terms of explicit Christian faith and tangible membership in the Church.

On the other hand it might also be possible to argue that the answer given by so many theologians today—that visible membership in the Church provides "an easier way of salvation"—represents little more than a practical adaptation of the extreme, and now untenable, position taken some years ago by Leonard Feeney, an American Jesuit, who "pertinaciously and publicly upheld the strict and literal interpretation of 'Outside the Church, no salvation'."[16] Should we not try to move radically away from such a position?

Hans Küng, with his usual clarity and force, has shown that the ecclesiocentric approach to this question—in terms of the negative proposition "Outside the Church, no salvation"—will always yield an answer that is not good enough: an answer that is inevitably regarded, among those on the "outside", as naïve and incredible. This theologian insists upon the urgency of removing the equivocations still associated with the Church's position: "An honest answer to

[16] *Ibid.*, p. 102.

28

the question has to be yes or no, not yes *and* no."[17] But this is invariably the perplexing sort of reply we must give when our starting point is the "little flock", the "insignificant minority", who actually constitute the juridical Church, outside of which "there is no salvation". So, Küng asks:

> Can you keep on saying this when you look realistically at the *future*, and consider that statistics show that non-Christian nations of Asia and Africa are numerically going to far out-strip the Christian nations of the West? That merely to preserve numerical relationship, there would have to be, not (as is the case) 500,000 converts to the Catholic Church each year, but 6,500,000? That it has been calculated that, by the year 2,000, China alone may number 1,700,000,000 people, which is 400,000,000 more than the present population of Europe, the Soviet Union, North and South America and Africa combined? What have you to say about the innumerable millions and billions who are going to live in the *future* outside the Catholic Church and altogether outside Christianity?[18]

If the usual ecclesiocentric starting point leads to no satisfactory answer, then there should be no fear of saying so, loudly and clearly. If an unambiguous statement on this matter "seems to diminish missionary zeal", then we must simply admit that some missionaries in the past were probably driven by a rather naïve apostolic purpose.[19] Is it too much to say that even Francis Xavier seems to have been mistaken on this point? If further theological investigation of this topic causes some missionaries to "feel uneasy" about the possible "damping effects" on apostolic zeal, then cer-

[17] Hans Küng, in *Christian Revelation and World Religions*, p. 33.
[18] *Ibid.*, pp. 27 f.
[19] Cf. *Mission & Grace*, vol. III by Karl Rahner, s.j. (Sheed & Ward, London, 1966), pp. 5-15.

tainly it is time for an honest re-appraisal: a radical and re-
solute re-examination of current missionary aims and
motives, with particular reference to the universal reality
of saving sanctification outside the visible structures of the
Church.[20]

Further reflection on the implications of "anonymous
Christianity", in relation to the corporate character of salvation in the existing historical condition of redeemed
humanity, suggests that the answer to the missionary question will not be found primarily in terms of making salvation "easier", or "more assured", for an ever increasing
number of men. Even these verbal formulations have a
curious and disturbing connotation with reference to the
workings of grace. Are we still, to some extent, haunted by
the Stoic asceticism of a British monk who lived in Rome
around the year 400?

Pelagius, aided by a Roman propagandist named Celestius,
initiated the idea that grace makes it possible to perform
good actions "more easily". The Christian, according to the

[20] For some samples of recent Roman Catholic re-thinking along these
lines, see the quarterly review *Teaching All Nations*, vol. IV, no. 1 (Jan.
1967): "The Meaning of Salvation and the Missionary Apostolate" by Yves
Congar, O.P.; and vol. IV, no. 2 (April 1967): "Mission, Dialogue and
Witness" by Josef Neuner, S.J.; "The Problem of the Absolute in
Christianity" by Joseph Ratzinger; "The Missionizing Church in her
Attitude towards the Non-Christian Religions" by Arnulf Camps, O.F.M.
These articles together amount to a comprehensive, intelligible and convincing statement of the present missionary question; when it comes to
an answer, however, they amount to something less. While Yves Congar,
for example, presents a clear case for a "new examination of the motives
that one can discover for the need of missionary activity", his actual
"examination" is marked by a disconcerting ambiguity in which missionary evangelization seems to become functionally identified with
Christian ecumenical collaboration in the field of socio-economic development on behalf of the non-Western world's poor masses whom the
Church is supposed somehow to "civilize" while evangelizing. The precise connotation of the word "civilize" in this context is not explained;
and an answer to the question of missionary motivation (for the establishment of the Church among these peoples) is hard to discover in this
otherwise interesting and informative "examination".

original Pelagian viewpoint, has "better means" of attaining salvation than the non-Christian; so it becomes "easier" for Christians to be saved. If pagans can achieve salvation through the exercise of their natural human virtues, then "imagine", wrote Pelagius, "what the Christians can accomplish, whose nature and life has been outfitted for better actions by Christ."[21]

Can we repudiate the Pelagian premise, and retain the practical conclusion that salvation is "easier" for those within the fold, because "better means" are available to them? The missionary question is still being answered by some theologians in such astonishing terms as these:

> If Christ set up the sacrament of repentance for the remission of the sins of Christians already baptized, it was because of the difficulty man experiences in accomplishing an act of charity. We know, in fact, that the act of charity justifies even without the sacrament. If, then, it is so difficult for the Christian, who knows God and has at his disposal all the means of salvation set up by him, to accomplish an act of charity, we must say that this difficulty is far greater in the case of pagans, who are deprived of these means and have often such an imperfect knowledge of God. We have to conclude that salvation outside the Church is possible, but more difficult.[22]

This curious coincidence of terms may not be in itself a sufficient reason for abandoning the "better means" and "easier way" approach to the question under consideration. But it should give us pause, and some inclination to search for another way of resolving the problem, while at the same time dispelling any suspicion that might arise with reference to anything like a crypto-Pelagianism. Indeed, an

[21] Cf. *Man and Sin* by Piet Schoonenberg, s.J. (Sheed & Ward, London, 1965), pp. 146-9.
[22] Domenico Grasso, s.J., *loc. cit.* (see footnote 5), p. 268.

entirely different viewpoint might serve us much better.

The missionary question itself must first be removed from any context of mathematical calculations and mundane measurements. It is "definitely impossible to apply the yardstick of average human reason to the glorious mystery of divine love in souls", as Piet Fransen tells us: for, "the action of grace lies outside our experience. . . ." This is why, Fransen continues, "we cannot draw divine action into the field of psychological and anthropological tests." Even the external norms of morality will not do as an adequate basis of comparison: "grace moves in the depth of the heart".[23] God's love is not determined by the psychological and anthropological difficulties experienced by His beloved.

There is another reason why the answers so far given are just not good enough. Even if the missionary commitments of the Church everywhere were so increased and intensified that the present rate of baptizing adults could be doubled annually, the explicit people of God will continue to be a progressively diminishing remnant in relation to the spectacularly increasing world population, especially in areas where the Church does not even exist. Islam alone, among other religions of the world, would still be growing in numbers more rapidly than Christianity. So the question would remain concerning the universal efficacy of God's love for all the others (an ever increasing majority of humanity), because of what the Lord of all has done also for them: "once and for all" (Heb. 9:26-28). Hence the Barthian question: "What hope is there for the others?"— for the multitude of the peoples in whose midst the New Israel is "only an inconsiderable minority"?[24]

[23] *Divine Grace and Man* by P. Fransen, s.j. (Desclée, New York, 1962), pp. 85, 88, 90, 91.
[24] *Christ and Adam* by Karl Barth (Collier, New York, 1962), p. 83.

The following considerations are therefore presented as *a different hypothesis*, another point of departure, for fresh approach to the meaning and the necessity of the Church, and of her missionary activity, for the salvation of each and every member of humanity. These thoughts are offered, moreover, with the profound conviction that missionary activity as such is *necessary* "today as yesterday: today more than yesterday".[25] So what is called into question here is simply some of the reasons which are sometimes given for this necessity. If the right thing is done for the right reason, we may hope that it will be done better.

[25] Pope Paul VI, *Address to the National Directors of the Pontifical Mission Aid Societies*, Vatican, 14 May 1965.

# II

## Anonymous Christianity

Theology has been led astray for too
long already by the tacit assumption
that grace would no longer be grace
if God became too free with it.

KARL RAHNER

Christians believe that Christ is the fully adequate representative of humanity before God and the truly comprehensive redeemer of mankind in its totality. The hope of Christians for the world is not merely an extension, through a
kind of pious fiction, of the hope they have for themselves.
It is rather the other way around. Christians have some
hope for themselves because of what Christ has done "once
and for all" (Heb. 9:26-28), as something positively decisive
for the whole of creation (Rom. 8:21-22; Col. 1:15-20; II
Peter 3:13). Apart from this whole there is no salvation for
Christians. They may be saved only through their participation in the one history of humanity, and in solidarity
with all the others who exist together with them in the
very same "second Adam" situation (I Cor. 15:22-28, 45).

All are involved together, whether each one knows it or
not, in one and the same saving destiny.[1] Every single
person, whenever and wherever he may live in history, is
intimately associated both with the lost vocation of the
"first Adam" and at the very same time with the vocation
of the "second Adam" in whom every one of them is given

[1] Cf. E. Schillebeeckx, O.P., *Mary, Mother of the Redemption* (Sheed
& Ward, London, 1964), pp. 61-2.

34

the essentially same potentiality for realizing the same common destiny of man in relation to God. This potentiality and its realization is what we call grace: redeeming grace. It is something given freely, without thereby abolishing the freedom in which it may be accepted or rejected, to undeserving men as the basis and the actualization of a new life of unity in the "second Adam". It is a gift to all men, gratuitously proffered by God to each one, on account of Christ in whom the whole of humanity is lifted up from the fallen condition of the "first Adam", so that mankind as a whole *has become* the people of God—although they are not yet manifestly, socially, juridically, and universally organized as such in the ecclesial symbol of this unity.[2] Such is the positive meaning of human solidarity in the One representative member who "*is* the whole of humanity", as Edward Schillebeeckx says so emphatically, "not simply in the juridical, but also in the real sense, even though this is possible only at a supernatural level."[3] Objectively then, every man is in the same initial condition: "already essentially redeemed in principle".[4] Such, in the eloquent language of Karl Barth, is the "ontological determination of humanity . . . grounded in the fact that one man among all others is the man Jesus. . . . He is the creaturely being in whose existence God's act of deliverance has taken place for all other men."[5]

Because of the "second Adam" situation in which all human beings exist, there is no such thing for any man as a *purely natural* life and destiny. Doubtless, God could have arranged things in such a way; but he did not. All men

[2] Cf. Karl Rahner, s.j., *The Church and the Sacraments* (Herder-Burns & Oates, London, and Herder & Herder, New York, 1963), p. 13.
[3] *Op. cit.*, pp. 63-4.
[4] *Ibid.*, p. 64.
[5] *Church Dogmatics* by Karl Barth (T. & T. Clark, Edinburgh, 1961), vol. III, 2, pp. 132-4; *Church Dogmatics: A Selection* (Harper, New York, 1962), pp. 166, 167.

belong only to the one existing supernatural order which is inundated and permeated and oriented by grace, and in which no man without grace has even a hope of attaining his final destiny. The basic premise of the argument, as set forth by Schillebeeckx, is this: "the present universal order of human existence is a supernatural order: man is created for Christ (Col. 1:16); no fully human personal moral orientation is possible without immediately being implicitly an orientation for or against the *Deus Salutaris*."[6] And Father Karl Rahner expressed it even more precisely in these words:

> Actual human nature is *never* "pure" nature, but nature in a supernatural order, which man (even the unbeliever and the sinner) can never escape from; nature superformed (which does not mean justified) by the supernatural saving grace offered to it. And these "existential facts" of his concrete (his "historical") nature are not just accidents of his being beyond his consciousness but make themselves apparent in his experience of himself. . . .[7]

In such a situation man is constituted, and transcendentally differentiated from the rest of mundane creation, precisely in his freely given capacity for grace as God's self-communication. "Man is man", wrote Paul Tillich, "because he is able to receive a word from the dimensions of the eternal."[8]

In this economy, however ambiguous the realm of human freedom may be, and in spite of man's consistently ambivalent exercise of freedom, God's gift of grace in Jesus Christ is much more effective unto life than are all of man's sins unto death. "The free gift following many offences brings justification. . . . So from the justice of the one the result

---

[6] *Christ the Sacrament* by E. Schillebeeckx (Sheed & Ward, London, 1963), p. 7.
[7] *Nature and Grace* by K. Rahner (Sheed & Ward, London, 1963), p. 35.
[8] *The New Being* by P. Tillich (Scribner's, New York, 1955), p. 121.

is unto justification of life to all men. . . . Where sin increased, grace abounded all the more. . . ." (Rom. 5:12-21; 11:32). "Once and for all" Christ appeared for the destruction of the sins of all (Heb. 9:26-28): one man standing adequately "for all" (II Cor. 5:15), "the just one for the unjust" (I Peter 3:18).

So it is that God, from the fullness of His unconditioned generosity, "enlightens every man who comes into the world", giving to each one "grace upon grace" (John 1:9, 16). And all of this without partiality (Rom. 2:11)! Indeed, He may be found even by those who do seek Him, as He has appeared openly to those who have made no inquiry of Him (Rom. 10:20). Why so much? Why go to such extremes? Because God Himself, on account of Christ, truly wills the salvation of all men (I Tim. 2:4), and He does not delay in His promises, lest any should be lost (II Peter 3:9).

In the light of this scriptural witness, and considering how relatively few men have been actually confronted with the explicit Gospel message, and mindful of the truth that the magnanimous ways of God—which are not the ways of men—are largely hidden in the depths of divine wisdom (Rom. 11:33; I Cor. 2:7, 12), it follows that "grace works for the most part anonymously. . . ."[9] God's unceasing concern for the world which He makes and remakes with no less ease, as also His ever active interventions in history, are concealed in the darkness of faith; and so they are always subject to misinterpretation by men who would try to measure, and to place logical limits upon, the magnanimity of God. But His greatness is not less beyond the borders of Israel (Mal. 1:5)—the new Israel as well as the old:

"Ethiop or Israelite, what care I?" the Lord says. "God that

[9] K. Rahner, *Mission & Grace*, vol. 1 (Sheed & Ward, London, 1963), p. 91.

37

brought you here from Egypt was God that brought the Philistines from Caphtor, brought the Syrians from Cir!" (Amos 9:7)

Surely then, if grace works for the most part anonymously, and all grace is always and only the same grace of Christ, we may speak of an "anonymous Christianity", an authentic life of grace (and not entirely hidden), among those whose historical situation makes it impossible for them to have more than an implicit faith in Christ.

Now this is not just some "modern theory" conjured up in order to explain away the widespread disobedience of Christians with regard to the Lord's final command that they should summon His disciples out of every nation.[10] Nor is it merely an ingenious ecumenical gimcrack manufactured by "progressive theologians" and offered to the non-Christian world, as a token of the Church's new "policy of appeasement"—acquired only since the discovery that Christians exist now in "a diaspora situation" where they are vastly outnumbered by all "the others". Rather, it is an ancient belief of Christianity, rooted in Scripture, as we have suggested above, and clearly formulated as far back as the days of Justin Martyr (c. 100—165) who expressed it in these unmistakable terms:

> It is our belief that those men who strive to do the good which is enjoined on us have a share in God; according to our traditional belief they will by God's grace share His dwelling. And it is our conviction that this holds good in principle for all men. Christ is the divine Word in whom the whole human race share, and those who live according to the light

---

[10] Matt. 24:14; 28:19; Mark 13:10; 16:15; Luke 24:27. Yet, less than five per cent of the Church's total endeavour in the world is presently committed to the evangelization of the peoples (some two-thirds of contemporary mankind) for whom the Church has never existed. Cf. "The Missionary Task of the Church" by Eugene D'Souza, *Council Speeches of Vatican II* (Paulist Press, Glenn Rock, N.J., 1964), pp. 281-2.

of their knowledge are Christians, even if they are considered as being godless.[11]

Other great names of the early Church are also associated with this sympathetic and optimistic application of St. John's Logos theology: Irenaeus, Clement of Alexandria, and Origen. Before as well as after the historical advent of Christ, and aside also from the presence of the Lord in the faith and sacramentality of His chosen little flock, the divine Logos is universally present to the whole of creation and in every person, as a germinating seed: a source of the goodness and light which is undeniably found among "pagans" of all times and places.

The various historical developments, formulations and presentations of this notion may be questionable in many aspects. Obviously they have been subject to misunderstanding and even to mischievous interpretation. But the basic insight belongs to pristine Christianity. This is why it has endured through the centuries, in spite of certain astonishingly crude statements that have been made in this connection by some of the Church's official servants.

About eighteen hundred years after the days of the Buddha Siddhartha Gautama, Pope Boniface VIII decided, in A.D. 1302, to "affirm and profess without qualification" that "outside the one and only Catholic Church there is neither salvation nor the remission of sins." As though this were not enough, he continued: "Furthermore, We declare, say, define, and pronounce that it is a matter of absolute necessity for salvation, for every human creature, to submit to the Roman Pontiff."[12] We know that this pontiff, who annulled all the official acts of his immediate predecessor

---

[11] *Apologia*, I, 10, 46; quoted in *The Kingdom of God Today* by Otto Karrer (Herder & Herder, New York, 1964), p. 11.
[12] *Denzinger's Enchiridion Symbolorum*, Editio 29, Herder, Friburg in Brisg., No. 469.

and then confined him for safe keeping until death, was trying mainly to assert his "divine" jurisdiction over kings; so he was concerned more with the political than with the theological implications of his statement.

In their single-minded insistence on the necessity of Church membership, the Fathers of the Council of Florence announced to the world (to their world of 1438-45) that "no one remaining outside the Catholic Church, not just pagans, but also Jews or heretics or schismatics, can become partakers in eternal life; but they will go to everlasting fire . . . unless before the end of life they are joined to the Church."[13] How can this sort of thing be explained? Professor Richard Drummond, in his very concise and well-documented summary of this whole question, says that such a statement must be understood only within its own proper historical context: Christendom's cultural isolation for a thousand years or so.[14]

Even the outstanding thinkers of this long period, innovators like Thomas Aquinas (who considered this matter briefly but positively),[15] imagined that the Gospel message had already been adequately presented to most men; so this was not for them a theological problem of high priority. The Council of Trent, in any case, made the necessary qualifications by recognizing a valid form of Church membership through desire.[16] And a number of Catholic theologians kept pushing for a more optimistic attitude towards those who were outside the Church through no fault of their own.

[13] *Ibid.*, no. 714; *The Church Teaches* by the Jesuit Fathers of St Mary's College (B. Herder, St. Louis, 1955), no. 165, p. 78.

[14] Cf., *Prolegomena to a Theology of the Christian World Mission* by R. H. Drummond, PH.D. (The Theological Seminary of the University of Dubuque, 1966).

[15] Cf., *The Church as Mission* by Eugene Hillman, C.S.SP. (Herder & Herder, New York, 1965; Sheed & Ward, London, 1966), pp. 90-1, 98; and "Christ Was There First" by Fulton J. Sheen, *World Mission* (Summer 1966), vol. 17, no. 2, p. 12.

[16] *Denzinger*, 796.

Notable among them: the Jesuit Father Ripalda and his contemporary, Cardinal Juan de Lugo (1583-1616).[17]

About three centuries later—and some twenty-three hundred years after Gautama—Pope Pius IX gave a realistic commentary on the meaning of "Outside the Church, no salvation". Up to then, Origen's negative formulation of the idea, and Cyprian's juridically exclusive interpretation of the axiom, seem to have been generally and uncritically accepted, at least on the level of ecclesiastical officialdom. But Pius IX, in this matter, had something positive to say: "It must likewise be held as certain that those who are affected by ignorance of the true religion, if it is invincible ignorance, are not subject to any guilt in this matter before the eyes of the Lord. Now, then, who could presume in himself an ability to set the boundaries of such ignorance, taking into consideration the natural differences of peoples, lands, native talents, and so many other factors? . . . The gifts of heavenly grace will assuredly not be denied to those who sincerely want and pray for refreshment by the divine light."[18] This was to be, presumably, the final and definitive statement of Christianity on the subject: "to proceed with further investigations", the pope added, "is wrong."

The general outlook of Catholic theologians on this subject in the period just before the Second Vatican Council was expressed typically by Karl Adam and by Abbot Vonier, in a tone which now sounds too apologetical and overly subtle. Father Adam spoke of those who may belong only to the "soul" of the Church, through an "invisible union" with the "supernatural soul and substance" of the visible

---

[17] For a general historical survey of Catholic thought on this question, see *The Salvation of the Unbeliever* by Riccardo Lombardi, s.j. (Burns & Oates, London, 1956); and for a more extensive current study of the whole question, see *Theological Investigations*, vol. II, Karl Rahner (Darton, Longman & Todd, London, Helicon, Baltimore, 1963).

[18] *The Church Teaches*, nos. 174 f., p. 81; *Denz.*, 1647 f.

Church.[19] While he regarded the Church as the "ordinary institute" of salvation, he went a bit far when he said that "alongside" the Church there are "extraordinary ways of salvation" through which the grace of Christ may visit particular men "without the mediation of the Church".[20] Regardless of the dubious phrasing, the insight is the same as Justin's. Vonier, in his discussion of this visibly *"extra ecclesiam"* condition of the vast majority of human beings, thought of their coming into the Church, "unconsciously, as one who is purified through influences whose origin he does not know."[21] And Pope Pius XII, in his encyclical letter on the Mystical Body of Christ, explained this necessary bond "by some unconscious yearning and desire".

Just in passing it might be noted that these various articulations of this idea of an "unconscious" Christianity were not looked upon as any kind of a threat to the missionary zeal of the Church. For Vonier, of course, missionary work was not simply a matter of converting to the Church as many people as possible anywhere and everywhere simultaneously. It was for him, as it is in the several mission encyclicals and in the decree of Vatican II on missionary activity, primarily and properly a matter of planting the

[19] *The Spirit of Catholicism* by Karl Adam (Sheed & Ward, London, 1929), impression of 1948, p. 202.

[20] *Ibid.*

[21] *The Collected Works of Abbot Vonier*, vol. II (Burns & Oates, London, 1952), p. 122. Cf., also *The Meaning of Grace* by Charles Journet (Paulist Press, Glenn Rock, N.J., 1962), pp. 139 ff., where the same matter is treated under the heading of "the fourth existential state of divine grace" through which non-Christians may become part of the Church in "a rudimentary and restricted fashion", by means of "uncovenanted Christian graces" which are "Christian graces by derivation" and superior to "Christian graces by anticipation" given before the historical coming of Christ. Whosoever responds to grace, without any explicit knowledge of Christ, is thus joined to the Church "spiritually" but not "corporally". Such persons are "hidden allies and accomplices" of the Church which "begins" to acquire through them . . ."a certain visibility".

Church where it has not been before.[22] "The salvation of souls", he wrote, "is a very definite kind of work: it is salvation through the Church; let the Church be established and souls will be saved".[23] There would be much less confusion about missionary motivation today, if everyone would put the emphasis where it should be: on the primary aim of establishing the Church on firm and indigenous foundations among the peoples who have "not yet" known Christ in this living community of Christian faith among them.

Now our rough historical sketch may be concluded with one more significant indication of the authentic Catholic position regarding the salvation of non-Christians. The ironical predicament of Father Leonard Feeney, who put himself juridically outside of the Church by his insistence on the literal necessity of empirical membership for everyone else (see above, p. 28), provoked further official clarification of the Church's teaching on this matter. At last it was said unambiguously that "to gain eternal salvation it is not always required that a person be incorporated *in fact* as a member of the Church, but it is required that he belong to it at least in *desire* and longing. . . . When a man is invincibly ignorant, God also accepts an *implicit desire*, so called because it is contained in the good intentions of soul by which a man wants his will to be conformed to God's will. . . ."[24]

So the notion of "anonymous Christianity" is not some "dangerous novelty" recently introduced into Catholic theology. It is rather a contemporary reformulation, in appropriately meaningful terms, of what Christians have always

[22] *Ad Gentes*, no. 6; where also the clear distinction is maintained between missionary activity as such and that pastoral activity which is exercised among the peoples for whom the Church has already been established.

[23] Vonier, *op. cit.*, p. 124.

[24] *The Church Teaches*, nos. 274, 275, p. 120, italics added.

believed and variously expressed, or sometimes not expressed. A very similar notion appears in current Protestant theology, particularly in Paul Tillich's description of Christian missionary activity by which the Church works "for the transformation of its own latency into its own manifestation all over the world. . . . The transformation is one from the Church in its latency, in its hiddenness under the forms of paganism, Judaism, and humanism, into its manifestation. This refers not only to the nations and groups *outside* of the Christian nations but also the Christian nations themselves. . . ."[25]

Now all of this does not amount to saying that the "latent Church", or "anonymous Christianity", embraces co-extensively every single person who lives visibly outside of the Church. Anita Röper, however, in her brilliant inquiry into this question,[26] does show how—with appropriate explanations—every human being may be regarded as a Christian in one way or another. But the really important point in this whole discussion is contained in St Augustine's well-known saying that many who appear to be outside of the Church are truly inside, and many who seem to be inside are really outside.

While we may have a firm hope in our salvation, and in that of all men, God alone knows who actually responds to His offer of saving sanctification, which most certainly is offered to men outside as well as inside the visible structure of the Church. Those on the outside who respond to grace, which is always the grace of Christ, may be regarded as

[25] "Missions and World History" by Paul Tillich, in *The Theology of the Christian Mission*, Ed. by G. H. Anderson (SCM Press, London, 1961), pp. 283, 285; see also *Church Dogmatics*, II-2, p. 418, where Barth speaks of "this concealed and dormant people of God in the world".

[26] *The Anonymous Christian* by Anita Röper (Sheed & Ward, New York, 1966).

"anonymous Christians". They belong to Christ through His grace; so they are joined in some real manner, although not juridically, to the Church. In the words of Father Schillebeeckx:

> God is the sole judge of man's conscience. One does not therefore affirm that all non-Christians are by the mere fact implicitly Christians, just as one does not maintain that every member of the Church is an authentic Christian. . . . An anonymous Christianity is a genuine possibility; and, considering the abounding power of grace, a reality in the case of many. We do not wish, nor are we able, to affirm their number. We know well the essential ambiguity of human freedom. . . . But our confidence in God is greater than that ambiguity. . . . The redemptive grace of 'Christus Victor' is more powerful than the fragility of human freedom.[27]

Finally, it should be noted that the discussion in this chapter, indeed throughout this book, is directed towards those who regard themselves as Christians. We are trying to see the condition of non-Christians simply from the viewpoint of Christian revelation; so the terminology used is relevant for the self-understanding of Christians in relation to the others. The matter could be looked at from the opposite side, and explained from the viewpoint of one who does not regard himself as a Christian in any way, either implicitly or explicitly. Then the terminology used should be rather different; for we are not trying to persuade them that, whether they know it or not, whether they like it or not, they are really Christians whenever they are following their consciences in good faith. This would not be very convincing to them; and, in their eyes, it might even appear to be just the same old "triumphalism" in a new disguise.

[27] "The Church and Mankind" by E. Schillebeeckx, *Concilium*, vol. I, no. 1 (Jan. 1965), British Edition, pp. 49, 50.

# III

## The Common Way

Once again—it is necessary to repeat,
because so many stupid things have
been said on this subject—on the
plane of personal conversion of heart
*there is no difference* between the one
who must find God outside of the
Church and without the sacraments,
and ourselves.
PIET FRANSEN

Every man has already, through the same grace of Christ, the real possibility of consummating the same positively saving relationship which the whole of humanity has with God on account of One Man. If final salvation is a real possibility for all men, *simply because they are men*, then the same life of grace, without which there can be no salutary orientation of one's earthly existence, is no less available to all of them by reason of the same universal mercy of God.

This precisely is the good news of Christian revelation: that saving-sanctification, for the fulfilment of our common destiny, is actually available to men whenever and wherever they may experience their brief participation in human history. So the real possibility of accepting this grace is equally authentic for all. The fact that most men do not have this message of hope explicitly announced to them does not make it any less true in their regard. A man's explicit belief in it adds nothing to the superabound-

46

ing efficacy of God's eternal love for what He has so generously made from nothing.

With this recurring theme of his, Father Rahner has cut sharply through the ambiguity of centuries: "If it is to do justice to holy Scripture, theology must say, and it generally forgets to say, that God has actually promised this efficacious grace for history as a whole and its single end (which can be viewed as the final result and the one meaning and pattern of all human history)."[1] This includes much more than the history of the "little flock" who have lived for the most part in Europe and the Americas during the past several hundred years; and so the sacramental actions of the Church also imply far more than the conferral of grace on those who participate explicitly in these ritual enactments.

"When we say," again with Rahner, "that Christ on the cross merited incontestably and irrevocably the 'grace of God', that grace is not only to be understood as a 'possibility' of effecting redemption, as a mere offer of attaining forgiveness and producing works of eternal life. That grace, viewed in relation to the totality of the history of the world and mankind, is a grace which effects the acceptance of what it offers; for, of course, all is grace: the possibility and the realization of the possibility, the capacity and the act, the word of God and the answer of man."[2]

"As it is, we do not yet see everything in subjection to Him . . . by whom and for whom all things exist" (Heb. 2:8, 10). "For we walk by faith and not by sight" (II Cor. 5:7). But we believe that God communicates with the whole of humanity in the tangible terms of mundane history and through the flesh of the Son of Man in whom all things are reconciled and recapitulated. For this very purpose

[1] K. Rahner, *The Church and the Sacraments*, pp. 16-17.
[2] *Ibid.*, p. 17.

the eternally saving Word Himself came forth in time from creation itself (Isa. 45:8). He came through and for that which, from the beginning to the end, He creates and recreates with equal ease. "For it was fitting that He, in bringing many sons into glory," should also bring His original work of their salvation into its historically visible completion by means of His actual sufferings in time and place, "even tasting death for every one", so that all might be recognized as His "brothers" (Heb. 2:9-11). If the "good news" is nothing less than this, then we will do well to search out its fuller implications in relation to the *oikumene*.

Is it not also out of the depths of created nature (especially through what we call "conscience"), and through the historical situations in which each man finds himself faced with concrete moral decisions, that the Word of God is spoken to each? For all men, these are the real moments of their encounter with God and of their deliverance from the captivity of sin. For man's response grace is needed, but not a preacher. (Most communication is, of course, non-conceptual.) This dialogue is man's destiny, given by the mercy of God: and this is the acceptable time of his salvation. Is this not the meaning of Rudolf Bultmann's eschatological vision of man, standing in the "crisis of decision" and under the judgment of God; and thereby manifesting precisely the essential characteristic of his humanity in the realm of freedom: man, standing alone before the Logos in the eternal "now" which is also his last hour, standing under the demands of a free decision for God and against his own congenital selfishness?[3]

This is the call to genuine altruism: death to the self for the sake of life with, and in, and for the other. These

---

[3] Cf. *History and Eschatology—The Presence of Eternity* by Rudolf Bultmann (Harper, New York, 1957), ch. X; also *Jesus and the Word* by Bultmann (Scribner's, New York, 1958), p. 131.

are the moments in which God moves man freely to become what he is, by obediently accepting God's word through the witness of the human conscience, however conditioned this witness may be by historical circumstances (Rom. 2 : 15); for even the particular boundaries of a man's personal history are determined by God for His own good purposes (Acts 17 : 26-27). For such encounters grace is authentically available to every man. Otherwise, we should be forced to conclude that Christ is not truly the saviour of the whole world: that the universal salvation proclaimed by Him is in fact a deception.

So the very same grace through which inner conversion is made actual for Christians of good will is no less available to non-Christians of good will: on this plane *"there is no difference"*.[4] And if there are degrees of holiness among the visible members of the Church, then these same degrees must be actual as well among those who, because of their historical situation, cannot have explicit faith in Christ. The cause is the same, and so is the sanctification which is effected by God's gratuitous and universal love for His creatures who are made in His image, not individually but collectively or corporately.[5] Salvation is not just for, not even especially for, those who happen to be born in the right time and place; it is for the whole of humanity. God's love is not frustrated by the rather late advent of Christ in history, nor by the notable lethargy of Christians in announcing this signal event among the nations.

The invisible reunion of all men in the Second Adam transcends and permeates all the circumstances of different

[4] Cf. "Theological Implications of Liturgical Discussion at the Council" by Piet Fransen, s.j., *The Church: Readings in Theology*, p. 188.

[5] Rom. 5 : 12-21; I Cor. 15 : 22-23; *Constitution: Lumen Gentium*, no. 9: "God, however, does not make men holy and save them merely as individuals. . . ."; see also Hillman, *The Church as Mission*, pp. 104-7.

times and places. The reconciliation of all, which is progressively accomplished from the beginning to the end of time through the hidden workings of grace everywhere among men, is not something less than the effective manifestation of this unity in the Church among the nations. Nor is the intensity of God's love for any man determined initially or finally by the external moral correctness of any actions performed by this man—especially when he may never have heard of all the "correct" things that theologians have deduced from Christian revelation. According to their respective historical circumstances, and the different means available to each of them, the ritual works of both Cain and Abel were externally correct expressions of faith. But only one of them—and this because of his hidden faith—did an acceptable work (Heb. 11:4; I John 3:12). Hence, Daniélou's comment on this: "The righteous man is not he who conforms his conduct to what is right but he whom God recognizes as righteous. . . ."[6]

The objective redemption of mankind in the flesh of the Son of Man is the supreme historical act and manifestation of God's redeeming love for humanity. All the rest, whether before or after, whether manifest or not, is a participation in the effects of this act which, because of its divine source and universal intent, is at once trans-historical: unbounded by historical space-time. The Church in history is therefore something less than the totality of what it signifies sacramentally: something less, that is, than the whole invisible reality of God's effective love for all men. The explicit people of God are the historically tangible "first fruits" of redemption, but they are not the only fruits. They are the representative part chosen to stand for the whole. The Church is not yet the fullness of God's kingdom, but the

[6] *Holy Pagans of the Old Testament* by Jean Daniélou, s.j. (Longmans, Green & Co., London, 1957), p. 30.

sacramental pledge of its invisible presence among all who respond to grace. The Church is the palpable instrument and the eschatological sign of the historical coming of the kingdom, now and at the end.

May we therefore permit ourselves to imagine that God loves the visible members of the Church more than He loves "the rest of men"? The final answer to this depends, of course, on how we understand the historical vocation of the explicit people of God: whether it is a calling of privileged favouritism for their own comfort, consolation and salvation; or whether it is the much more risky business of being chosen primarily to serve God's purpose in clearly specified ways among men, with personal holiness being a kind of gratuitous concomitant of obedience to this vocation.[7] For our immediate purpose here, the question may be put otherwise: Does God love His creatures less effectively before, and after, manifesting His love in the Incarnation, and through the sacramental continuation of this mystery in the life of the Church among the nations?

It is not that men love God because they see the historically tangible Christian manifestation of His love for them. It is that "He has first loved us" (I John 4 : 10), and then sent His Son to be significantly present among men through the Church's extension in different times and places. It is precisely because He so comprehensively loves the world that He sent this witness in the "latter days" for a sign to be raised up among the peoples, showing them in human terms the love with which they are first loved, from the beginning to the end.

This witness is given within the limited dimensions of time and place among one people after another, but it testifies to an eternal and all-embracing love which is just as effective before and after its historical manifestation

[7] Cf. chapter 7, footnote 22.

in the flesh of Christ and in the sacramentality of the Church. The sign is an effective glimpse of the signified reality which was concealed, but was not ineffectual, for ages; and which only now is being progressively disclosed in order to bring about obedience to faith among the nations (Rom. 1:15; 16:25-26; Eph. 3:4-11; Col. 1:26-27).

Because of what Christ has done in the sight of men the Christian view of mankind's destiny is optimistic. We may not place human measurements against the magnanimity of God. "We have no right," as Rahner puts it, "to assign arbitrary limits to the grace of God outside the Church. . . ."[8] Yet there are some Christian writers today who tell us, quite definitively, that the number of those who may "perhaps" be called "anonymous Christians" are a "very small minority".[9]

Should not our attitude be rather that the prayers and good works of all men, whether they are Christians or not, have generally the same intrinsic value before God, with any "degrees" of value being determined solely by the intensity of God's love for this or that particular person? For these prayers and good works are made possible and actual only by God's grace which is given only through His Son who is recognized at least implicitly in every human reply to God's word; and because grace itself is the ultimate measure of the value and the dignity of any prayers and any good works. Since we are quite incapable of evaluating the intensity of God's love for any man, we must normally

[8] *The Dynamic Element in the Church* by K. Rahner (Herder-Burns & Oates, London, Herder & Herder, New York, 1964), p. 64.

[9] Cf. Van Straelen, *op. cit.*, p. 108. While he does not defend the extreme position taken by Feeney, this particular writer seems very annoyed to see the pendulum moving now in the opposite direction; so he has undertaken to warn us, in rather shrill but theologically unimpressive tones, against "three contagious diseases which", he imagines, "are at present rampant in many parts of the world." These are: "ecumenitis", "dialogitis", and "salvationitis" (pp. 95 ff.).

assume that one's external attitude of prayer and one's outward posture of charity proceed from a right inner disposition, which is right only when caused by grace.

We know that Christians may act hypocritically; as, for example, when participating in the Eucharistic communion while remaining consciously attached to serious personal sin. But, because of our trust in the victorious power of grace we do not consider this hypocritical attitude to be typical of Christian behaviour. Nor, for the same reason, should we consider it typical of non-Christian conduct—unless we are prepared to assert that redeeming grace is not authentically given for the actual salvation of the majority of redeemed mankind. The fact is, as we learn from the Gospel and we know from experience, that Christians really are "like the rest of men" (Luke 18:11). All are sinners, always in need of God's grace without which no man has even a hope of responding to the call of his human destiny in the present supernatural order. All human behaviour is a persistent reminder not only that all men are sinners in need always of God's mercy, but also that He actually gives His grace abundantly to all, whether they are Christians or not, whether they reflect explicitly on this or not.

The well-known story of a priest, a Levite, and a Samaritan on the road leading down from Jerusalem to Jericho is a universally relevant myth. That is to say, it is not a "fairy tale" but a symbolic way of expressing a universal situation which is immediately comprehensible to all men of any time and place. It is a primordial and ever recurring human predicament which calls for a right human response through a free decision to die to one's self for the sake of another, to go out of one's self because of the needs of another. And this, as we have seen, cannot be done without grace which operates "for the most part anonymously". The details of this incident on the way to Jericho show also something that most of us have probably learned from our own experience and observation: that those who have been called and chosen for the professional service of God's revealed religion do not respond to grace more easily or more frequently than anyone else.

Everyone, from time to time, experiences the demands of such a situation which may be expressed in countless ways. The witness of conscience does not require verbal formulations and Hellenic concepts. Situations speak for themselves: "I was hungry, and you . . .". Man's conscious reflection and explicit motivation are not mentioned here by the Lord, and they are clearly beside the point in these cases of ultimate judgment. Explicit knowledge of Christ, and conscious reference to Him, are not required for a person's salutary response to the offer of grace in and for these decisive situations: "Lord, when did we see you hungry, or thirsty, or a stranger, or naked, or sick, or in prison; and when did we . . .?" (Matt. 25:24-46).

No one is forced internally to respond as he ought, but the positive response (and who would dare to say that this is not common among non-Christians?) can be made only under the influence of grace which so permeates this present order of human existence that its effects are apt mistakenly to be regarded as "purely natural"—as though unaided human nature were capable of genuine altruism:[10] "And

[10] Cf. K. Rahner, *op. cit.*, pp. 54, 63: "The Church teaches that even the lasting observance of the natural law, that is, what belongs to the accomplishment of human nature as such in the world, requires a special help from God which in fact, ultimately speaking, men only receive from the grace of Christ. Consequently even the preservation of purely human moral excellence points, objectively speaking, to the power of grace. . . . It is quite possible to hold that as a matter of fact in all or nearly all cases where a genuine spiritually and morally good action is actually accomplished, it is also, in fact, more than merely such an act."

everyone who loves is born of God, and knows God. . . .
No one has ever seen God. If we love one another, God
abides in us and His love is perfected in us. . . . God is love,
and he who abides in love abides in God, and God in him"
(I John 4:8-16). It is precisely in this law of love that all
of the other means of salvation are summed up, contained
and fulfilled (Rom. 13:8). And, of course, the Spirit of
love breathes freely where He wills.

It is not merely in temples made by human hands, and
through rituals devised by human minds, that man decides
to respond to his destiny in relation to his neighbour and
his God. He decides on the road and in the market place.
Intentions are formed and aspirations are expressed in the
churches, in the temples, and in the groves; but the really
decisive encounters are commonly made elsewhere. Indeed,
it is above all in situations of fraternal service, concretely
offered, that the gift of salvation is actually bestowed on
any man.[11] God offers fulfilment to all men in these events
which break in upon us, interrupt us, disturb us, and demand
from us a decisive answer.

Dietrich Bonhoeffer put his finger on this exactly. This
is why his message rings so true in our age of impatience
with the dusty accretions of previous centuries. He saw the
fulfilment of human destiny, through these moments of
salvation, offered directly in terms of these "interruptions
by God" who is "constantly crossing our paths and can-
celling our plans, by sending us people with claims and
petitions".[12]

The scope of the question before us is as wide as the
history of human experience. It is only in the light of this
total perspective that a satisfactory answer may be found.
For we are concerned at once with the position of the

[11] Cf. E. Schillebeeckx, in *Concilium, loc. cit.,* p. 36.
[12] *Life Together* by D. Bonhoeffer (SCM Press, London, 1954), p. 89.

visible people of God in relation to God's saving love for the whole of His redeemed humanity. Up to now, and in the foreseeable future, only a relatively small (and now progressively diminishing) segment of mankind can be counted among the Church's explicit members. And more than ninety per cent of them are presently found within that one third of the world's population, living in Europe and the Americas. It might be added—to dramatize the question —that they are, for the most part, white. Now are these explicit people of God really given "more opportunities of salvation", so that they may be "more easily" saved than all the others? Are they, because they participate consciously in the sacramental life of the Church, "more sanctified" and, therefore by implication, "morally better" than the rest of men?

Authentic opportunities for accepting grace are, as we have seen, copiously offered to all men in and through the daily events of mundane existence. It is on this level, above all, that the salvation of each man is worked out in the same condition of "fear and trembling". These gracious occasions, inviting men to serve their brothers, and asking them to die to themselves through obedience to conscience, are so frequent that no one is able consciously and reflectively to cope with all of them. Under the myriad disguises of different times and places the same situations recur with the same persistent demands for a right human response in terms of fraternal service, involving some degree of death to the self for the sake of the other. Such are the common predicaments of salvation and the most decisive occasions of grace, without which no man is able to transcend his own congenital selfishness by the donation of himself in fraternal service.

If the life of each man is thus inundated with these grace-proffering events, then the occasions for loving God through our neighbour are not presented more frequently to Christians than to the rest of men, nor are they presented in a more decisive manner. And certainly these acts of genuine fraternal love do not appear to be less common among non-Christians, any more than wickedness seems to be more common among them.

Indeed, these occasions are nothing less than the initial and common and indispensable and final way of salvation for all men, and the only available way for most men. God alone knows whose love is made right by the grace of Christ who is truly offered to all men in a living faith which may be either implicit or explicit, depending on each one's historical situation as assigned to him by providential circumstances beyond his own control.

It should be remembered that we are not speaking here about the case of an individual who is explicitly called from "paganism" (or from a condition of "anonymous Christianity") to become a visible member of the Church. If such a person's conscience, after an adequate confrontation with the Gospel message, directs him to become an explicit Christian, then obviously his personal sanctification and salvation are immediately and directly involved with his obedience or disobedience to the call. As a result of a positive response to his conscience, he may be thought of as being in a "better" condition than *he* was before this latest act of grace-inspired obedience to his conscience; but, as regards the possibility of his attaining final salvation, he is not necessarily in a "better" condition than his brother who has not been so directed by his own conscience. What we are concerned with in these pages is the situation of those who, through no fault of their own, are not adequately presented with the Gospel and the call to visible membership in the Church: most of humanity, that is.

Regarding all that is comprehended in the theological

notion of "anonymous Christianity" ("implicit faith", "baptism of desire", "hidden allies of the Church", "the latent Church", etc.), we may therefore say with Schillebeeckx that "these are not an extraordinary way of grace but the initial stage—something which of its nature requires to grow to completion—of the ordinary and universal mode of the bestowal of grace."[13] This whole hidden, but none the less living, world of "extra-sacramental" grace must be, and is being, completed by the historical visibility of the sacramental Church among the nations; for all grace is, in the end, sacramental. And the Church exists in order to manifest this universally.

So it is not by the accidents of historical time and place, when and where a man happens to be born or reborn by the Holy Spirit, that one is given *a priori* a better or worse chance of salvation. Nor is it because of one's personal historical vocation—whether a priest, a Levite, or a Samaritan—that one is more apt than another to respond to the offer of grace. The opportunities are commonly, and indeed overwhelmingly, available to all, by reason of the universally victorious and superabounding grace of Christ. As God is no respecter of persons in the dispensation of His merciful love, neither is He constrained to favour the men of those particular times and places in which His mercy is temporally and tangibly manifested by the presence of Christ, whether in His historical flesh or in His sacramental community.

Does it not also follow that the citizenship of heaven is made up largely from that vast majority of human beings who did not belong juridically to the Church on earth? The parable of the workers in the vineyard is surely relevant here (Matt. 20:1-16): God is not unjust because His generosity, by human standards, seems too great. In such

[13] *Christ the Sacrament*, pp. 178-9.

an economy of love the last are apt to be given the first place; the inheritance may not be given to the first born; the barren wife may bear seven sons while the mother of many languishes; and those who think that they stand should not be so sure of themselves.

# IV

## The Other Religions

We shall have to face it in our time . . .
Christianity has never answered Symmachus.
ARNOLD TOYNBEE

Quintus Aurelius Symmachus, a spokesman for the
ancient Roman Senate, was an eloquent apologist for the
moribund culture-religion of his ancestors. He is remembered today, and briefly mentioned in manuals of church
history, for having exchanged theological debating points
with a better-known contemporary of his, St Ambrose of
Milan. Symmachus was a "pagan", and he lost the argument. It was too late anyway for him to have expected a
serious hearing. Well before his death "in the year of the
Lord" 410, Christianity had become the official religion
of the Empire, with all other religions being proscribed.
Shortly thereafter non-Christians were excluded even from
holding public office. But one of the points made by Symmachus remains with us still. Concerning the mystery of
the universe and of human destiny, he inscribed these words
on a long-lasting parchment: "It is impossible that so great
a mystery should be approached by one road only."[1]

Christians have not yet considered deeply, extensively,
positively, and in the light of their own faith, the significance of the religions that have always served the majority

[1] Cf. Arnold Toynbee, *Christianity among the Religions of the World*
(Scribner's, New York, 1957; O.U.P., 1958), pp. 111-12; *An Historian's
Approach to Religion* (Oxford University Press, New York, 1956), pp.
253, 297, 299.

of human beings, and will evidently continue to serve an ever-increasing portion of redeemed humanity, possibly even until the *eschaton*. The initial efforts and the major contributions in this field of study have been made more by social scientists than by theologians. But things are changing. Christianity is now facing the question raised more than fifteen centuries ago by the Roman senator.

Efforts are being made in our time, as never before, to answer Symmachus who spoke for a much larger world of other religions than either he himself, or his adversaries, realized. Does it still sound "offensive to pious ears" to hear a modern Dominican friar teaching that "pagan" religious rites manifest "an anonymous but none the less effective operation of grace"?[2] Catholic theologians really have come this far, and there is no turning back. Even before the recent Vatican Council, Father Schillebeeckx was teaching that "'natural religion', based on that which the unaided human spirit can achieve of itself, is a fiction. . . . In the concrete, all religions presuppose an at least anonymous supernatural revelation and faith."[3]

The unprecedented attitude of Vatican II on this subject is just a beginning, an official opening of the question. "In our time," the Council Fathers declared with due modesty, "the Church is giving deeper study to her relationship with non-Christian religions."[4] It is now recognized officially that the Church *is* in a relationship with every other religion, because she is the servant of all "who acknowledge God, and who preserve in their traditions precious elements of

[2] E. Schillebeeckx, *Christ the Sacrament*, p. 7.
[3] *Ibid.*
[4] *Declaration: Nostra Aetate* (On Non-Christian Religions), Vatican, 1965, no. 1; cf. also *Declaration: Dignitatis Humanae* (On Religious Freedom), no. 6; *Constitution: Lumen Gentium*, no. 16; *Decree: Ad Gentes*, no. 22; *Constitution: Gaudium et Spes* (On the Church Today), no. 92.

religion and humanity."[5] It is now appreciated that "the other religions, to be found everywhere, are striving variously to answer the restless searchings of the human heart, by proposing 'ways' which consist of teachings, rules of life, and sacred ceremonies."[6] Since the Church regards herself primarily as an instrument of God's historical revelation of Himself to the whole of mankind, she desires now, and publicly asks for, "frank conversation—to compel us all to receive the inspirations of the Spirit faithfully, and to measure up to them energetically."[7] Such is the exhortation addressed to the present generation of Christians. It is a call to "dialogue and collaboration with the followers of other religions".[8]

If this call has come rather late in the history of the Church, it is, for that very reason, all the more urgent. The official servants of the Church have not always perceived so clearly that Christianity exists primarily for the whole world. Most men are still quite oblivious of this, as they continue to follow the religious ways of their forefathers. And, also, most Christians seem equally blind to the implications of their own historical position in relation to the masses who have never explicitly encountered Christ in any significantly intelligible way. What does the Church mean to her own members in this second half of the twentieth century after Christ; and what is her meaning for the greater part of the *oikumene*? Even the self-understanding of Christians will be largely shaped by the answer they give to the question raised by Symmachus. But the answer does not come easily.

Christianity's reply cannot be given simply from the top, merely by professional theologians and Church leaders. It

[5] *Gaudium et Spes*, no. 92.
[6] *Nostra Aetate*, no. 2.
[7] *Gaudium et Spes*, no. 92.
[8] *Nostra Aetate*, no. 2.

must also be worked out gradually on the ground level of actual human existence, where the living encounter takes place between Christians and their brothers who do not believe. A well-demonstrated response to the question, with all of the appropriate references and footnotes, may be intellectually convincing to a small group of interested scholars; but wide acceptance is hard to achieve against an historically conditioned and emotionally coloured background marked by centuries of intolerance, cultural isolation, spiritual arrogance, and mutual suspicion. The difficulties involved in the dialogue among separated Christians are compounded in the wider ecumenism under discussion here.

Even today the particular religion of a man is usually determined for him *a priori* : by the accident of his birthplace, by obscure historical events, or by current political situations. Most men are not sufficiently free to choose for themselves which road they should follow in order to concretize and fulfil their inner religious aspirations. They tend quite uncritically, and in good faith, to accept the way of their fathers : the way of their culture-religion, whatever it may be. For them, "a meridian decides what is the truth", as Pascal said. Are they wrong for doing this? Will the religious situation of most men ever be otherwise?

A disconcerting element in the "scientific" study of religions has been the terminology used, and the evolutionary cast of thought. In the superior manner of nineteenth-century Europe, there was just too much thought of "religion from that of savages up to that of civilized man", as Edward Burnett Tyler expressed it.[9] And Andrew Lang's incredibly neat category of "high gods and low races" is apt to put one off immediately from pursuing his thought any further.

[9] Cf. *The Beginnings of Religion* by E. O. James (Hutchinson-Arrow, London, 1958), pp. 9-27.

Charles Darwin's brilliant reflections in the realm of biology seem to have been far too literally and uncritically applied to the order of human culture and social organization. The whole of life was supposed to fit into Herbert Spencer's dictum: "from the simple to the complex. . . ." And, of course, everything would work out in Comte's "law of three stages". It would seem to follow "scientifically" from this that certain Western intellectuals, who think this way, would be standing on the higher cultural rungs of this convenient ladder of their own imaginations, and looking down upon the monotheistic "savage races" of the lowest rungs.

This sketch may be too much of a caricature. It is intended merely to point out the limitations of some otherwise valuable studies which are more recent but still marked by perhaps too much reliance on suspiciously clear layers of stratification: too much cultural progressivism, "from the lower to the higher", with Western man always on the top. Theologians could well dispense with such thought-patterns, as they consider simply the content of various religions. At least at the present stage of theological inquiry into the other religions, it should suffice to see them as differing from one another: not as "higher and lower". Otherwise, there could be some prejudice to the case of the tribal religions in comparison with the "more developed" and more complex religions of Buddhism, Jainism, Islam, Hinduism, Shintoism, etc. Degrees of complexity in thought and organization are not necessarily related to degrees of value and of truth.

Without having first to become an expert in the content of the various religions, it is possible for one to theologize intelligently about non-Christian religions as such. It might even seem better to maintain the distinction between the sociological study of religions and the Christian theology of religions. "The essence of all religions", wrote Jacques-Albert Cuttat in his discussion of this very point, is like the nature of human love which "will inevitably escape us, as long as we consider it only as nonparticipant spectators. . . ."[10] So, he continues:

> Either I observe with a certain detachment the whole complex of the various concrete religions, so as to explore them scientifically as so many phenomena, and in that case I am incompetent by definition, since the object of my study becomes not the very essence of religions, but only their anthropological, philosophical, psychological or historical residua or accessories. Or else, my viewpoint being properly religious, I possess the required competence, and I will then necessarily approach the various creeds from and through one of them, namely my own, failing which I would lack both knowledge and authentic spiritual experience.[11]

In this way, Cuttat concludes that the more deeply one goes into his own religion, the more he becomes capable of "penetrating and assimilating the core, the really positive content, of other religious perspectives."[12] This, in general, is the manner of approach chosen by Father Rahner, and followed subsequently by Professor Heinz Robert Schlette in his effort to carry Rahner's thought somewhat further.

Among Catholics the ground was cleared for a positive evaluation of non-Christian religions only in the recent past. This was a result of the stormy controversies, dramatically associated with Henri de Lubac's return to the authentic Christian tradition in *Surnaturel*, which finally set in order the relationship between the natural and the supernatural.

[10] *The Encounter of Religions* by J. A. Cuttat (Desclée, New York, 1960), p. 15.
[11] *Ibid.*, p. 16.
[12] *Ibid.*, p. 31; for a similar view, see *The Faith of Other Men* by Wilfred Cantwell Smith (Mentor, New York), pp. 80-1.

Rahner's contribution to this work of ground-clearing seems to have attracted less attention,[13] possibly because those who caused de Lubac's discomfiture, by their critical misrepresentations, did not perhaps read German.

What the so-called "new theory of the supernatural" established—and it is widely accepted today—was this: that there is no such thing for man as a "purely natural" human existence in history, because man actually exists only in a supernatural order, with a final destiny which cannot be attained without grace. As Dom Illtyd Trethowan recently expressed it:

> The modern theologian's "state of pure nature" (held commonly in 1947) is not only unhistorical but inconceivable . . . for the being called *man*. . . . De Lubac's purpose, in fact, was to show that the gratuitousness of God's activity in our regard, and in particular that aspect of it which produces "the supernatural order", is properly preserved only in the ancient and genuine tradition, obscured in recent centuries, according to which man has only one end, which he cannot attain without the grace of God; he has not, and never has had, a natural end. . . . God's creation of man and his "ordering" of man to the supernatural end were equally gratuitous for the simple reason that they are two ways of talking about the same thing.[14]

This understanding has constitutive importance not only for the following reflections but also for all that has been set forth, with references to the working of grace, in the previous pages of this book. Against such a background, and considering the social nature of man as well as the incarnational tendency of grace, it appears quite normal and providential that *homo religiosus* should "everywhere strive

[13] Cf. K. Rahner, *Theological Investigations*, vol. 1, pp. 377-97.
[14] "The Supernatural End: P. de Lubac's New Volumes" by Dom Illtyd Trethowan, *The Downside Review*, vol. 85, no. 277 (October 1966), pp. 397, 398.

variously—by proposing 'ways' which consist of teachings, rules of life and sacred ceremonies—to answer the restless searchings of the human heart."[15]

Given the long and wide absence of Christianity in concretely experienced human history, after as well as before Christ's visible coming in the flesh and in the sacramentality of the Church, it is not surprising that the inner workings of grace among men everywhere and in all times should lead to socially external expressions of morality, concrete ritual situations, and corporate acts of worship, with indigenous cultural roots among the peoples who constitute humanity as a whole. To simply deny the salutary significance of these forms and structures would approximate a denial of the social and religious nature of man, and even a denial of the universality of grace.

May we assert that a purely individualistic and formlessly interior response to grace is normal among men, and appropriate for all but Christians who themselves insist so much on the essentially social nature of their own religion? Not if we believe that salvation is a corporate affair, that redeemed man is a collective being, that one may be saved not simply as an individual but only as a member of the human race, and that this solidarity can be expressed only within the cultural context of one's own community of historical existence—not in some other community that is present to one only as a mysterious intangibility. Once the general validity of non-Christian religions has been acknowledged, then Rahner's conclusions become unavoidable.

"By legitimate religion we mean," in Rahner's words, "an institutional religion whose 'use' by men at a given time can be considered on the whole as a positive medium of the proper relation to God and thus of obtaining salvation, and as such is positively taken into account in God's saving

[15] *Nostra Aetate,* no. 2.

plan."[16] The substantial arguments for this notion need not be reproduced here, as the Council Fathers of Vatican II have already recognized the social validity of all genuine religions;[17] and hence, their legitimacy for all who adhere to them conscientiously. So we may conclude with Rahner that "if man can always have a saving positive relationship with God, and if he has always had to have it, then he has had it precisely within the religion actually at his disposal as a moment of his existential milieu."[18] And once again:

> The divinely intended means of salvation for the individual meet him within the *concrete* religion of his actual existential milieu and historical contingency, according to God's will and forbearance (which so intermingle that they are no longer clearly separable).[19]

The fact that a genuine religion as such is a legitimate instrument of grace for men in a given historical situation does not mean that any erroneous or depraved elements, which may be found in that religion, are sanctioned by God. The weeds and the wheat are permitted to grow together until the end (Matt. 13:29-30). Every religion, and not only those which are extra-biblical, is impure in its concrete historical embodiments. All socio-religious forms and structures belong to fallen humanity, so they are marked by the sin, the frailty, and the shame of man.

Religions in themselves, interpreted and administered as they must be by sinners, are instruments of grace, but at the very same time they are also manifestations of sinful man's need of grace. So each religion always requires purification of itself through the repentance of its most faithful

---

[16] *The Church: Readings in Theology*, p. 124.
[17] Cf. *Lumen Gentium*, no. 16; *Sacrosantum Concilium*, no. 37; *Gaudium et Spes*, nos. 58, 73, 92; *Optatam Totius* (On Priestly Formation), no. 16; *Ad Gentes*, nos. 11, 12, 26; *Nostra Aetate*, nos. 1, 2, 5; *Dignitatis Humanae*, nos. 1-15.
[18] *The Church: Readings in Theology*, p. 128.     [19] *Ibid.*, p. 129.

followers. This implies the humble and honest self-criticism of religious men who must be forever adapting and reforming the human elements of religion, in obedience to the inner movements of grace which is denied to no one.

Even the biblical religions of Judaism and Christianity, in so far as they must be expressed through human institutions, have within them their own man-made stumbling blocks to salvation. We need only recall the mission of Israel's prophets, or the condition of the Jewish religion in the time of Christ, and the exacting religiosity of the Pharisees: those precise followers of revealed religion. And what was the common Christian attitude for centuries with regard to the institution of slavery? St Augustine said it was "a punishment for sin. . . . And this is why the Apostle (Eph. 4:5) admonished slaves to be subject to their masters. . . ."[20] While economic forces within Christendom were transmuting slavery into serfdom, St Thomas Aquinas coolly declared that "slavery among men is natural. . . . Between the master and his slave there is a special right of domination", including the master's right to beat his slave.[21] We might also think of the "purely pagan character of Baroque religion", which prompted Father Louis Bouyer to remark that "the Baroque period was Catholic through an instinctive loyalty to the Church, although it was not genuinely Christian."[22] And what religion today, including the quasi-religions of humanitarianism and Marxism, is without stain? On this level all religions have much in common: human stupidity, hypocrisy, self-righteousness, superstition and very earthy wickedness. As Vahanian says in *The Death of God*: "Our religion is as crude as that of the fetishist."

[20] *The City of God*, Book XIX, ch. 15.
[21] *Summa Theologiae*, IIa-IIae, q. 57, aa. 3 & 4, q. 65, a. 2.
[22] *Life and Liturgy* by L. Bouyer (Sheed & Ward, London, 1962), pp. 5-9, 42-44, 52.

This point about the limitations of organized religion has been driven home rather forcefully in recent years, thanks very much to the prophetical voices of men like Karl Barth and Dietrich Bonhoeffer; and, alas, very much to the shame of Christians in our time. But the message has come through, thanks to Pope John and so many others of his kind. So, once this has been understood with due humility, it would seem superfluous now to go with Barth and Bonhoeffer, or rather with their latter-day interpreters, "beyond religion".

A purely cerebral de-mythologizing process, that conveniently ignores man as he is actually extended throughout the whole of concrete history, leads only to a kind of neo-angelism; and thence to that atheism which is an anti-concept born legitimately from Christianity's marriage to Western abstractionism. Christian faith cannot live as an abstraction. The Christian message of salvation is, on account of Christ, incarnational: its communication requires external human forms and social structures. This is the only way that men, as historical and social beings, can continue to grope together towards what is beyond. Western philosophy may dispense with religions and their feeble efforts to express the inexpressible; but men will not give up; and most men do not live in the West.

However inadequate any religion may be in its concrete historical situation, the grace of God remains the same, as does the nature of redeemed humanity. So the real possibility remains equally valid for every man to respond, through grace-given obedience, to the witness of conscience, however conditioned this witness may be by historical circumstances (Rom. 2:15). Even these circumstances are determined by God for His own good purposes (Acts 17: 26-27). No religious structures are more important than the men for whom they exist, nor are these external means more salutary than the inner movements of grace, and the longing for God, which they are supposed to signify effectively.

Religions, of themselves, do not save men; but they do make men conscious of their need for salvation. And opportunities for accepting God's offer of personal communion (even if non-conceptual) are surely provided through the good and positive elements in all religions: through "whatever is true, whatever is honourable, whatever is just, whatever is pure, whatever is lovely, whatever is gracious" (Phil. 4:8). Every religion serves God's saving purpose in history, in so far as it offers men an awareness of their own inadequacies before God—even when God may be only a suspected influence behind the immediate questions of human destiny. Every religious act is a saving act, in so far as it directs men to a greater love for one another.

This is not a matter of saying that one religion is as good as another in guiding men along the path that leads to final salvation. For a start, we do not even have reliable data for making sweeping generalizations concerning the comparative salutary and humanizing value of the countless religions of mankind. (It is hard enough just trying to understand our own.) Some of the grand theorizing in this field must therefore be taken with considerable reservation.

Some of the "precipitate comparisons and identifications" made by Mircea Eliade are, for example, highly questionable;[23] and so are some of his methods of gathering and verifying data.[24] And, if such a brilliantly objective observer as Arnold Toynbee seems to betray a somewhat inadequate grasp of his own native religion, then how deeply has he understood "the others"?[25] Lacking the divine perspective

[23] Cf. *Towards a Theology of Religions* by H. R. Schlette (Burns & Oates, London, Herder & Herder, New York, 1965), p. 53.
[24] Cf. *Patterns in Comparative Religion* by M. Eliade (Sheed & Ward, London, 1958), pp. 138, 142, 203; the data and judgments here referring to the Masai people of East Africa seem quite erroneous to me.
[25] Cf. Schlette, *op. cit.*, pp. 87, 138, n. 48.

required for judging comparatively the intrinsic value of each religion, we may say simply that each one is a different historical means by which God may communicate Himself to men through whatever is good in them.

According to Professor P. Idiart of the French National Centre of Research, "each religion is like a language, or more accurately like a tongue, codifying the methods of exchange in a particular historico-cultural pattern."[26] This view is worth considering further. Idiart continues:

> We cannot understand and compare religious phenomena from the outside, as objects, by reference to their historical environment, or to their place in a given structure, without seriously misreading them and distorting their meaning, if we do not bear in mind that they express a purpose, that they are not objects but signs, referable to a signified before being capable of correlation.[27]

What do all religions strive to signify? On analysis from "within", it might be found that the commonly and constantly signified reality is the "Wholly Other", and the exigencies of human nature in relation to this presence. And what can Christians hope to achieve through a mutually interpenetrating dialogue with the followers of other religions? Initially, it is certain that they can arrive, through such an exchange, at some deeper understanding of their own faith. Beyond this, we shall have to wait and see what further possibilities may be hopefully opened—the possibility perhaps of mutual completion in one another, as Raymond Panikkar has suggested.[28] But we are still at the preliminary stage of wondering what our own Christian faith may have to tell us about our relationship with the

[26] "The Priest, Pagan and Christian" by P. Idiart, in *The Sacrament of Holy Orders* (Liturgical Press, Collegeville, 1962), pp. 261 f.

[27] *Ibid.*, p. 262.

[28] Cf. R. Panikkar, in *Christian Revelation and World Religions*, pp. 168-9.

others. We are just now examining the basic elements of our hopeful theology of religions. And so we may now turn to a brief consideration of what Professor Schlette has contributed towards this.

The existing non-Christian religions of the world, in their "pre-Christian" historical setting, constitute an "ordinary" way of grace, while the Church is an "extra-ordinary" way. In Schlette's view, which is not his alone, these religions are not to be considered as "pre-Christian" simply in the order of chronological priority. Rather, they are seen as theologically prior to Christianity, and in terms of the here and now historical experience of countless millions of religiously concerned human beings among whom Christianity is neither known nor accessible in any adequately historical manner.

Since this is the real situation of the rapidly increasing majority of human beings, and considering the commonly accepted meaning of words, it does make sense to say that non-Christian religions provide an "ordinary way of salvation", while the Church provides an "extra-ordinary way". [29] The point is made clearly enough through such a use of words, provided the biblical sense of the term "way", in this same thought context, is not forgotten. There really is only one way : Christ in whom man's faith may be, with equal validity for salvation, either implicit or explicit.

Schlette's argument hinges decisively on the difference between *general* and *special* sacred history. These are "two aspects of one and the same occurrence of the history of divine epiphany which at the same time is always the sacred history of redemption."[30] General sacred history is based on the theological meaning of the covenant with Noah : concluded with *the whole of humanity*. This is a universal,

[29] Schlette, *op. cit.*, p. 81.
[30] *Ibid.*, p. 93.

cosmic, and everlasting alliance made with "every living creature on earth" (Gen. 9:8-17). Salvation is offered to all of them through the obedience of one of them (Gen. 6:18-22). Special sacred history, however, is based on the covenant with Abraham: concluded with *a chosen group of human beings*. This is a particular alliance made only with some men. This relates to all men ultimately, as the two histories (general and special) gradually converge in the course of time towards their culmination in the *eschaton*.

The real inner convergence comes about in the reconciliation of all things through the hidden operations of the grace of Christ in whom the promise to Abraham is actually being fulfilled always and everywhere among men who respond to grace. But this promise of blessings among all the families of the earth (Gen. 12:13) is outwardly symbolized in history only progressively, in the consecutiveness of historical time, by the living and indigenous presence of the Church among the nations. So general and special sacred history are becoming *visibly* one through the obedience of the Church to her original pentecostal mission (cf. chapter 7, p. 118).

Now something more must be said about the salutary significance of *general* sacred history. Alongside of the particularism of the Old Testament, the special concern with *the chosen people*, there is at the same time, even if it is less frequently dramatized, a constant stream of universalism: a consistent concern with all the nations of the earth, which "is filled with the steadfast love of the Lord" (Ps. 33:5; 119:64). In the New Testament the Lord Himself declares that the very same judgment, based on love that is given or not given with respect to the *real needs* of men, will be passed on all men, whether or not they recognize explicitly the special covenant sealed by Himself in history (Matt. 25: 31-45). And the Lord mentions specifically the tolerance of the judgment that will be passed on those living outside of the special covenant: the peoples of Tyre, Sidon, Sodom, and Nineveh (Matt. 11:21-24; 12:41). Many corroborative affirmations are found throughout the sacred writings.[31]

The entire biblical witness suggests that all who are subject to the divine judgment must be first under a covenant of God's merciful grace: if not the special alliance made with His chosen people, then that which was made first with all of His creatures. If St Paul could "liken the case of the pagans of his own day to those of primitive humanity previous to Abraham", as Daniélou has pointed out,[32] then we may say also that the unevangelized peoples of our time are still under the irrevocable and salutary cosmic covenant. The rainbow still appears in the sky.

The universally salutary covenant of general sacred history is valid for all men; and it is superseded only among those who *actually experience* special sacred history, through explicit faith within the community of God's specially chosen people: a representative people who are a part of humanity standing for the whole. This messianic people of God "does not actually include all men".[33] It is the "little flock". So we may say with Schlette that "the primary significance of special sacred history does not lie in the 'salvation of souls'. . . . The superiority of special sacred history, and especially of the Church, does not consist of a more advantageous chance of salvation."[34]

From the theological (not chronological) viewpoint, we who are Christians today stood first, in principle, "on the plane of general sacred history . . .".[35] But in the course of

---

[31] For a summary of the biblical evidence on this question, see Hans Küng, in *Christian Revelation and World Religions*, pp. 38-46.
[32] *Holy Pagans of the Old Testament*, pp. 14 f.
[33] *Lumen Gentium*, no. 9.
[34] Schlette, *op. cit.*, pp. 85, 93.
[35] *Ibid.*, p. 89.

history we were transferred "from the ordinary way of salvation to the special, not because we were or would be better than the rest of men, or so that we might attain salvation more easily; but solely because it pleased God to reveal His glory and at the same time the mystery of history, by the incomparable way of special sacred history; and because in this the lot of divine choice fell on us, in Christian terms, because God can act as seems good to Him."[36] Once again, by following a slightly different route this time, we arrive at the mystery of divine election, as expressed in the parable of the vineyard workers (Matt. 20: 1-6). The special vocation of God's chosen people is to be understood in this light.

Obviously it is not possible here to summarize all of the recent contributions that have been made on this vast, and still somewhat nebulous, subject. We are merely indicating the theological basis for the Christian's own self-understanding in relation to his current desire, and his long-standing need, to approach the followers of other religions; and to approach them in a manner that is both positive and sympathetic, while at the same time respecting the integrity of his own Christian vocation. One further quotation might serve to complete Schlette's thought on this capital point:

The Church, as the divinely willed society of those called, is not therefore as it were the privileged band of those who walk the wide and ordinary way of salvation while "the others" who "sit in darkness and the shadow of death" (Luke 1:79) are saved by God in some extraordinary way, if at all. The Church is rather the eschatological community, called together from the four winds, which by its existence in the world is to bear witness to the goal to which the ordinary way of salvation (the religions) lead, and which at the same

[36] *Ibid.*, p. 90.

time demands in the name of God that the extraordinary way should be followed in obedience and humility.[37]

In the historical perspective of mankind's salvation, we may say therefore that, regardless of the concrete religious structures which are, or are not, available to him in his own particular time and place, every man has an equally valid possibility of attaining final salvation through the superabounding grace of Christ. And, because of what Christian revelation teaches about the mercy of God, we may hopefully presume that God's self-communication through the hidden operations of grace is very much more than just a valid possibility for most men. But there is more to it than this; for *homo religiosus* does not exist merely as an isolated individual before God, but always as a member of God's beloved and redeemed humanity, and always together with others in a particular human society.

Since God speaks His saving word to men only in the terms of mundane history, and through the living experience of each man within his own cultural context and social milieu; since the message of Christianity is not presented explicitly to most men; since everyone is obliged to obey the dictates of his own historically conditioned conscience, which is of course always subject to further historical conditioning and enlightenment through grace; since *homo religiosus* has concretely available to him everywhere his own socially relevant religions, which his conscience urges him to follow; and since these religions, however ambiguous or even erroneous in many respects, contain good and positive and uplifting elements; then these various religions must be regarded as valid, and particularly significant, instruments of grace for those who adhere to them faithfully and in good conscience. All men are called

[37] *Ibid.*

to reunion with God through the life of grace, "but few are chosen" to be visible witnesses among the nations to the universality of this calling (Matt. 22:14; 26:28).

At the same time, each man, whether he is a Christian or not, is always free to disobey the dictates of his conscience, however clear or ambiguous the testimony may be before his conscience, and thus to reject the offer of grace. Ultimately it is God alone who decides about the final destiny of each. So there is much room for optimism: especially because of what God has done through Christ "once and for all" as an effective manifestation of His unbounded love for all men who are created and recreated "through and unto Him" in whom "all things hold together" (Col. 1:16-17).

Finally. If we wish to approach non-Christians in a truly humble and open manner, it would seem necessary first to understand fully, and to make our own, these words written on this subject by Father Panikkar:

We mean to say that this ontic mediatorship of Christ is independent of the religion an individual may profess, and from the place and time of his existence on earth, whether inside or outside Christianity, or within or without the historical existence of the visible Church. What Christ claims to be and to perform is valid for the Animist, Hindu, Muslim, etc., as well as for the Aztec, the Mongol, Greek, European, etc., as also for the Cro-magnon man, for those who lived 15,000 years ago or for the man of our time. If we lose sight of this catholic Christic perspective, we may easily falsify all relationship among Christians and the so-called non-Christians.[38]

[38] R. Panikkar, *loc. cit.*, pp. 164-5.

# Part Two

## THE SIGNIFICANCE OF HISTORICAL CHRISTIANITY

# V

## The Relevance of the Church

> Within its depths I saw ingathered,
> bound by love in one volume,
> the scattered leaves of the universe.
> *Paradiso*

In the course of stating the question about the necessity of the Church for the salvation of all men, in relation to the universally victorious reality of Christ's saving grace, we have seen that purely juridical concepts provide no reliable starting point for a satisfactory answer. For we are concerned here, both in asking the question and in seeking an answer, with the full mystery of the people of God, and with the very reason for their visible existence. This new messianic people is, above all, a sacramental community. As Christ is the sacrament of God, so the Church is the sacrament of Christ.[1] Any meaningful answer must therefore be found and formulated, first of all, in terms of sacramentality. All other considerations are consequent upon this.

Aside from this, all of the bell-ringing, organ-playing, hymn-singing, candle-lighting, incense-burning, water-pouring, bread-breaking, rule-keeping, cathedral-building, mitre-wearing, and crosier-bearing, have no more universal relevance than the spinning prayer wheels of any other tribal

---

[1] "The Church—the whole Church, the only Church, the Church of today and yesterday and tomorrow—is the sacrament of Christ; strictly speaking, she is nothing other than that, or at any rate the rest is super-abundance." *The Splendour of the Church* by Henri de Lubac, s.j. (Sheed & Ward, New York, 1956), p. 127. Cf. also *The Parish: Eucharistic Community* by Casiano Floristan (Sheed & Ward, London), p. 78.

religion. Even the kind deeds and the noble teachings of Christianity have their counterparts all over the world under different religious labels. But the Church aspires uniquely to relate all these things, both inside and outside of her visible structures: indeed, to reconcile them, to recapitulate them, to summarize them in herself. This she can do only through a universal sacramentality which comprehends the full dimensions of human history.

This is so, because of what the Church is: "Not simply the Church that is in this particular place," as St Augustine expressed it, "but both the Church that is here and the Church which extends over the whole world; not simply the Church that is living today, but the whole race of saints, from Abel down to all those who will ever be born and will believe in Christ until the end of the world, for all belong to one city. . . . This is the whole Christ: Christ united with the Church."[2] The whole history of salvation, from the beginning to the end, the entire drama of sin and holiness, might be recapitulated analogically, as a way of indicating the organic unity of God's comprehensive plan in which there is no "better" or "worse" time and place for man's acceptance of saving-sanctification, and for his free entrance into the one city of God's own people.

The Church, from the first man to the last who will ever respond to grace which works "for the most part anonymously", is already everywhere, both before and after its visible manifestations in the name of Christ. Since its sociological establishment at Pentecost, the Church will remain visibly on earth until the end. It will remain among some peoples, but we cannot say which particular peoples. Before God the first are last and the last are first, a thousand years are as one day, whole nations are like a drop of water in

<hr/>

[2] *In Ps. 90, sermo* 2, PL 37, 1159; quoted in *The Whole Christ* by Emile Mersch, s.j. (Bruce, Milwaukee, 1938), p. 415.

a bucket, and the islands are but a handful of dust. All men are equally distant from Him, and equally close to Him who is never far from any one of us. This is why the acceptable time, the day of salvation, for each man is always "now". That God may love this one more than that, we cannot say.

All men, whenever and wherever they may be in the consecutiveness of history, are related to one another and to their Creator with the equal necessity and the relative value of each note in a symphony.[3] What went before is no less significant for the whole than what follows. The individual sounds do not become more valuable as the symphony unfolds progressively towards its preconceived point of termination or fulfilment. The beauty and the fullness of all, as with the consecutive events of human life and history, are always and everywhere in the "now" of each sound which itself touches eternity, but only as a part of the whole in and for which each separate element exists and finds its full meaning. The effectiveness of what went before is derived from what follows, and vice versa. The Church of the "latter days" is not the totality of the reality, but the finale: the terminal summing up and the completion of all that is done, from the beginning to the end, by God's creating and re-creating Word. As Hans Urs von Balthasar put it: "All our destinies are interwoven; and until the last of us has lived, the significance of the first cannot be finally clear."[4]

It is against this background that we should consider the unique and necessary position, and the special vocation, of the explicit people of God in relation to the salvation of the world: They are called only *from* and *for* "the others". So it is only within this total perspective that we may hope to

[3] Cf. *Christianity and History* by Herbert Butterfield (Collins, London, 1957), p. 91.
[4] *A Theology of History* by H. Urs von Balthasar (Sheed & Ward, London, 1963), p. 73.

find the authentic motivation for our missionary work of planting the Church among the "tribes and tongues and peoples and nations" who have *not yet* seen the final sign of the world's salvation: the sacramental *Lumen Gentium*.

Obviously it is not possible in a single book to discuss fully all of the presuppositions, the points of reference, and the ramifications, which are necessarily involved in any effort to comprehend the inner nature of the Church. However, from the central consideration of the Church as the sacramental symbol of mankind's salvation, and perhaps only from this viewpoint, it should be possible to see the precise and prior goals of the Christian vocation in the organically related and eschatologically oriented history of salvation. It is in the dynamic element of this vocation that we will find the keenest incentive and the deepest motivation for the missionary activity of planting the Church among the peoples who have not yet known Christ in this sign raised up among them on firm and indigenous foundations. It is here that we will find the reason for the Church's historical existence anywhere at any time, and the relevance of God's explicit people for the salvation of mankind, and thus and only thus for themselves.

Our belief in the universally operative and mostly hidden reality of saving sanctification does not compromise, nor is it diminished by, the unique necessity of the Church for the salvation of each and every man. So the first question before us is this: In what sense are non-Christians, who respond to grace, related and joined to the visible Church without which there is no salvation?

We are of course speaking of those who, through no fault of their own, have not been adequately confronted with the Gospel of Christ, and have not been thereby called to explicit faith in Christ and juridical membership in the

Church. Theirs, we must recall, is the ordinary existential condition of the vast majority of redeemed humanity. Also included in this problem are countless Catholics and Protestants whose apparent relationship with Christ is exclusively juridical—often amounting to little more than a name in a baptismal register. We would agree with Congar that most of them are not Christians.[5] This suggests, just by the way, a more awkward question which each of us must answer for himself: "Are we?"

All things are being reconciled in Christ through the hidden operations of His grace always and everywhere among men. This inner reality is being progressively and effectively summed up and symbolized through the tangible presence of the Church among the nations in the consecutive terms of human history. Because of the gradually unfolding terms of this concrete history, in which salvation is taking place, the inner union of men with God and the real unity of the whole human race will be fully manifest to the eyes of flesh only at the end, after the universal mission of the Church shall have been completed in the sight of all peoples: "For before the Lord comes," as the Fathers of Vatican II remind us, "the Gospel must first be preached to all nations."[6] In the meantime, which is missionary time, this unity made by grace is signified only to the eyes of faith. It is outwardly accomplished only as a pledge of hope. And it is brought about only through the witness of authentic love.

The new people of God are saints and sinners who are called out of every tribe and tongue and people and nation. Their explicit union of faith and hope and charity is a living testimony of that reconciliation which brings order out of chaos, good out of evil, acceptance out of revolt, truth out of contradiction, and unity out of estrangement. The Church

[5] *The Wide World My Parish*, p. 93.
[6] *Decree: Ad Gentes*, no. 9.

is thus an effective sign of the universal brotherhood of men. Whosoever truly loves his brother loves Christ, even if he does not consciously recognize the unity of all men in this "first born" of many sons and many brothers. The reasons for this have already been proposed in the first part of our inquiry; and they may be summarized in these words of the Council Fathers:

> All men are called to be part of this catholic unity of the people of God which, in promoting universal peace, presages it; and, in various ways, there belong to or are oriented towards this unity both the Catholic faithful and all who believe in Christ, as well as all men in general since they are called by the grace of God to salvation.[7]

He who responds to grace is thereby joined in some real way to the Church. He is related to Christ as a brother, born of the same Father through grace; and so he truly belongs to the people of God, even if he has not been chosen to be a juridical member of the Church. As Pope Pius XII put it, in addressing an audience of midwives in 1951, "an act of love can suffice for an adult to obtain sanctifying grace and supply for baptism."[8]

While all men are called to salvation within God's invisible kingdom of grace, only a few are actually chosen to be explicit witnesses in the Church to the universal reality of God's saving love. It is an obvious fact of history that the Church's visible structure "does not actually include all men".[9] So it follows that "all" are not chosen for this particular historical vocation of witness within the Church. The explicit people of God are, after all, a "small flock". Indeed, in our own time, they are a progressively dimin-

---

[7] *Constitution: Lumen Gentium*, no. 13.
[8] Quoted by Congar, *op. cit.*, pp. 122-3.
[9] *Constitution: Lumen Gentium*, no. 9.

ishing remnant in relation to the rapidly increasing world population.

But they are the "remnant" of Israel renewed, with all that this word means in Scripture. So they are "a lasting and sure seed (a palpable pledge) of the unity, hope and salvation of the whole human race."[10] It is their unique vocation to be, in tangible union with Christ, just this: "a sign raised up among the nations, inviting all who have not yet believed".[11] This is a participation in, and a sacramental continuation of, the one mission of the Messiah who is "a signal beckoning to the peoples all around . . . high lifted up for a world to see it: the standard that shall call Israel home, gather in the exiled sons of Judah from the four corners of the earth" (Isa. 11:10-12).

The salutary significance of the community of explicit Christian faith is rooted in the Incarnation from which the Church, as the sacramentally symbolic continuation of this mystery in the extension of different historical times and places, derives her reason for existing, her meaning and necessity for humanity as a whole. All salutary acts are intrinsically related to their sources in, and through, the one historical Incarnation of the eternally saving Word of God. And they are thus related, in a subordinate mediatory manner, to the Church which Christ willed to be His own sacramental continuation among men: "He who listens to you, listen to me" (Luke 10:16). As Joan of Arc put it so simply to her learned judges: "It seems to me that it is all one, Christ and the Church, and that we ought not to make any difficulty of it."[12]

All the actions of hidden grace are destined, because of the incarnational structure of the present economy of salva-

[10] *Ibid.*, words added in brackets.
[11] Vatican Council I, Denzinger's *Enchiridion Symbolorum*, 1794.
[12] Quoted by Henri de Lubac, *op. cit.*, p. 125.

tion,[13] to explicit and universally social manifestation in the historical life of the Church among men. This is why the Church must continuously incarnate herself among one after another of the nations who, as distinctive ethnic-culture units of men, constitute the whole of mankind in universally relevant, natural, primordial and intrinsic symbolism. As the final stage of salvation history was initiated by the fleshy presence of God's Word "once and for all" (Heb. 9:26-28) in the history of humanity, so this saving process is being organically brought to historical completion by His sacramental presence "once and for all" in the particular histories of the peoples who are humanity in the extension of different times and places.

Christ stands as the one representative of humanity and the only mediator; and He is this precisely as man: "the Son of Man".[14] His representative and mediational character is sacramentally present in the Church through which His real presence remains, in palpable signs, among men. The explicit members of the Church are "gathered from the different peoples",[15] who constitute humanity in its spatio-temporal extension. They are gathered in order to stand with Christ as the sacramentally symbolic and historically

---

[13] In the existing human condition on earth all free human moral acts of love for God, or for one's neighbour, have a certain necessary incarnationalism, as they always manifest in some degree of historical tangibility the inner reality of love, and of grace, from which they proceed. So every saving act (even "outside" of the Church), because of its intrinsic causal relationship to Christ, has a quasi-sacramental character and relationship with the Church: Cf. *Theological Investigations* by K. Rahner (Darton, Longman and Todd, London, 1963), vol. II, pp. 85, 87; also *Christ the Sacrament* by E. Schillebeeckx (Sheed & Ward, London, 1963), pp. 47-54, on the necessity of this incarnational-sacramental prolongation of God's tangible self-communication through Christ; and pp. 56 ff., on the final and full externalization of grace, as the constitutive essence of the Church which is thus the visible realization and historical completion of the saving reality of grace.

[14] Cf. Schillebeeckx, *op. cit.*, p. 50.

[15] *Lumen Gentium*, no. 13. It is not whole nations as such that are called into this gathering, but men *from* every nation.

tangible representatives of all those others who live, have lived, and shall live the same life of grace anonymously.

Here it should be noted that everything we are trying to say about representation (the part standing for the whole in an organic unity with reference to the past and the future as well as the present) presupposes and hinges on the very important biblical notion of "corporate personality", as first elucidated by the British scholar Henry Wheeler Robinson,[16] and again more recently by the Jesuit Father Jean de Fraine.[17] While this is not a familiar category of Western thought, it does nevertheless seem essential for a deeper understanding of the biblical message concerning the people of God in relation to the scriptural "nations", and in relation to very much else besides. It is, moreover, an extensively experienced anthropological category outside the world of Western individualism; and, as such, its validity is recognized in the modern social sciences.

Very briefly, "corporate personality" is a highly functional and meaningful category in reference to the experienced human solidarity of social groups properly speaking. It does not refer, for example, to a gathering of blind people, or a mass of troops; nor does it apply to a group of workers in a factory. It is based rather on the intrinsic continuity and stability of bonds such as common origin and culture, involving a vital sense of shared destiny and mutual responsibility, reaching both into the past and into the future, with a fluidity of expression by which the destiny of the individual member is easily and naturally identified with that of the collectivity and vice versa. This implies the conviction, among many others, that "the present moment could be conceived as recapitulating the whole

---

[16] Cf. *Corporate Personality in Ancient Israel* by H. Wheeler Robinson (Fortress Press, Philadelphia, 1964).

[17] Cf. *Adam and the Family of Man* by Jean de Fraine, s.j. (Alba House, Staten Island, N.Y., 1965).

past, just as it could be conceived as pregnant with the whole future."[18] Such inner dynamics belong, in various degrees of explicitness and consciousness, only to the family, the clan, the tribe, the people, the nation, and to humanity.[19]

All of the biblical teaching about human solidarity and representation—humanity in Adam and in Christ, for example—is presented through this notion of "corporate personality". It is not easily translated into the terms of Western philosophy; but de Fraine has succeeded in doing just this, as in the following passage, for instance:

> . . . In the biblical category of "corporate personality" . . . causality is based on a prior and fundamental metaphysical unity. Because the group is one with the individual, the latter can express himself through this "extension of his personality", even after a considerable length of time. Unity (profoundly intrinsic) precedes causality (and always somewhat external). In a very concrete sense, the individual and the group together form one single reality whose structure can further expand in a relationship of causality. Basically the individual does not fulfil his role by representing the group, or even by influencing it for good or for bad; in the framework of "corporate personality" we can say very objectively that *he* is the group and that the group is *he*. When we come right down to it, we are here face to face with one of the most profound intuitions of biblical metaphysics; namely, the dynamic (not at all static) character of the idea of "being": the individual tends to become the group, and the group tends to be identified with the representative individual.[20]

Perhaps the best proof of the reality expressed by this concept, for those who require proof, is to live for awhile

[18] J. L. McKenzie, quoted by de Fraine, *op. cit.*, p. 24.
[19] For some further reflections on this, see Hillman, *op. cit.*, chapter IV: "The Nations".
[20] *Op. cit.*, p. 272.

among the members of an African tribe. "The proof," for Father de Fraine, "if there is one, lies in the universality with which the idea of 'corporate personality' seems to fit so many texts" of the Bible,[21] beginning with the first, and ending with the second Adam. At any rate it is well worth the effort to divest ourselves momentarily of our Western philosophical categories which tend to be excessively individualistic in relation to the meaning of man. Then we should be better able to see man in this less precise but more universal way: "Even if we experience a certain difficulty in accepting as our own this Semitic or Oriental mode of thought, rather than reject it, we should adapt ourselves to this scriptural category in which the divine Word has been clothed."[22]

Using this notion of "corporate personality", we may say therefore that the explicitly faithful members of Christ among a particular people are called to stand symbolically (in virtue of the biological, historical, and cultural continuity which makes a people one) for all among their own people who have known Christ, and shall know Him, only through the hidden operations of His grace, and through that implicit desire which theology recognizes as a form of baptismal incorporation in Christ. It is in this way that the Church is called to stand among each people, and for all men, as the socially present and unique representative of redeemed humanity. It is in this way, by striving with all of her energy and the grace of her primary vocation to raise herself up among the nations, that the Church is making up in the flesh of her members that which is still lacking in comparison with the sufferings already endured by Christ for the sake of all men. It is in this way that the Church does sacramentally once for all in each nation what Christ has done historically once for all humanity. The function is one of sym-

[21] *Ibid.*, p. 19.     [22] *Ibid.*, p. 273.

bolical representation, about which more will be said in the following chapter.

Since Christ is the "light of the world" and the "expected of the nations", the Church is sent by Him and with Him to all the peoples of the earth, as His sacramental epiphany in the consecutive and gradually unfolding terms of history. This is why the Church exists: to manifest Christ among the nations, and thus to summon from among each people God's chosen witnesses, not for themselves exclusively or primarily but for all the others.

Here is the reason for the existence and the special historical position of a chosen group of men both under the old and the new covenant. The primary meaning of their existence, as indicated by Professor Schlette, "lies precisely in (their) reference to the 'others', the 'gentiles', in fact to 'all' (Gen. 12:1-3; Isa. 45:20-23; Matt. 26:28; Mark 10:45; 14:24), and precisely on that account there is perceptible to the faithful in Israel and in the Church, and only to them, a 'lack', a deficiency, an 'inferiority' on the part of those others with whom, it must always be confessed in faith, God has concluded a 'covenant'."[23] And that which is still "lacking" in relation to the fullness of the sacramental body of Christ's witnesses is to be progressively made up by all of His existing members, as they donate themselves (each according to his place in the body) to the service of Christian witness among the nations for whom and from whom they themselves are called and chosen, in order that the incarnational plan of mankind's salvation might be brought to its historically signified completion.

Hence, the prior mission of the Church is this: to gather together "from the four winds" the new messianic people, the chosen witnesses, who are still scattered among the nations, and still sitting in darkness. They are to be sum-

[23] *Towards a Theology of Religions*, p. 74.

moned together so that they may become consciously and explicitly, in the sight of all men, the universal sacrament of mankind's inner unity and common destiny which are accomplished always and everywhere, in the first place, through the invisible operations of grace. So, the work of evangelizing the nations, by establishing the Church among them on firm and indigenous foundations, is not simply a means of extending and building up the Church in the world. Rather, the Church herself is a *means* of evangelizing the nations.

What of those, then, who have already seen this messianic light for which the majority of the peoples are still waiting? What is the first responsibility of those whose deliverance has already been signified to them through their membership in the Church raised up among their own peoples? The Lord replies through His prophet:

> I have an errand for them, to be my messengers across the sea: to Africa and to Lydia where men draw the bow, and to the islands far away.

> They shall go out where men never heard my name, never saw my glory yet, to reveal that glory among the nations.

> And out of all the nations they shall bring your brethren back. . . . And some among these newcomers, the Lord says, I will choose out to be priests and Levites (Isa. 66:18-21).

This vision of the Church's necessity for all men (or the Church's need to incarnate herself among all peoples) cannot be encompassed and expressed in the precise and literal phrases of canon lawyers. Efforts to answer the question on the purely juridical level—in terms of converting to the visible Church every single individual among one or another particular people, and thus forming homogeneously Christian nations—will get us nowhere. Such an approach to the mission of the Church is more reminiscent of the religio-political fantasies of the Middle Ages than of the Gospel message which sees the tangible reunion of all men in terms of sacramental symbolism, not in terms of their individual numerical computability. Even the neat and orderly formulas of medieval scholasticism have proven to be inadequate vehicles for the communications of this "mystery which has been hidden from eternity in God", and is now being made manifest in the Church, "according to the eternal purpose which He accomplished in Christ Jesus our Lord" (Eph. 3:9-11).

Scripture itself, while its message is based on the literal meanings of words and on God's actual interventions in concrete history, speaks of these things largely in the language of symbolism.[24] This means of communication is universally relevant, because it is intelligible to men of any time and place: the story of the good Samaritan, for example, or the countless references to the "whoring about" of God's chosen people and the eventual coming of the bridegroom in spite of what the Church, standing for humanity, has made of herself. It is in these terms that we must learn again to approach the mystery of the Church which is, after all, not the total reality of God's saving work in history, but the incarnational instrument and the eschatological sign of it: not the whole earth but the salt therein, not the whole bread but the leaven within, not the fullness of God's Kingdom but the pledge of it.

This primary notion of the new messianic people of God, as the "universal sacrament of mankind's salvation", is clearly and dramatically put before us in the dogmatic

---

[24] Cf. *Paul Tillich in Catholic Thought*, Ed. T. A. O'Meara, O.P. and C. D. Weisser (The Priory Press, Dubuque, 1964), especially the chapters by Gustave Weigel and George Tavard; *Myth, Symbol and Revelation* by Gerald Vann, O.P. (The Thomist Press, Washington, 1962), pp. 6-12; "Symbol, Myth and the Biblical Revelation" by Avery Dulles, S.J., *Theological Studies*, vol. 27, no. 1 (March 1966), pp. 1 ff.

constitution of Vatican II on the nature of the Church.[25]
The Church is constitutively this "sign among the nations"
in relation to the whole of humanity for whom she exists,
precisely because of the already actively saving presence of
Christ, the Word of God, in humanity.

While the explicit people of God in the Church of the
latter days are not actually, and cannot be in individual
numerical visibility, co-extensive with all of redeemed mankind from the beginning to the end of history, they are
nevertheless the authentic symbolical manifestations, and
in this representative sense the very reality itself, of God's
whole people "from Abel down to all those who will ever be
born" of grace into the life of implicit or explicit faith to
which all men are called. "This is the whole Christ" in
humanity "united with the Church" through grace. But
this reality has not yet been fully and efficaciously signified
by the Church whose historical mission has not yet been
completed in the extension of different times and places
among the nations. The Church exists in order to do just
this: to body forth herself in the sight of all men, that they
may see what she is, and what they themselves are: God's
beloved people.

So it is now possible to say, with Paul Hitz, that "the
radical and decisive basis for missionary work is not primarily man, humanity, or the idea of making salvation possible or easier; it is the Risen Christ Himself already present
in the Church and in humanity as a whole."[26] In order to
join the Church's activity in history with His own saving
presence in the world, and thus to signify His universal
presence, Christ calls and sends His chosen witnesses among
the nations. In this perspective, "the sacrament of the mis-

[25] *Lumen Gentium*, nos. 1, 9, 48.
[26] Cf. "Christ Risen, Humanity and the Church" by Paul Hitz, c.ss.r.
in *Lumen Vitae*, vol. XX, no. 4 (1965), English Edition, p. 605.

sionary presence of the Church",[27] necessarily involves the salvation of men for two reasons.

In the first place, Christians may hopefully expect salvation for themselves only through their obedience to the primary demands of the Christian vocation. They may be saved only by sharing with all men in the divine Agape from which they themselves, after the manner of the biblical "first fruits", are the first to benefit. Secondly, it is only through the tangible presence of the Church among the nations that the universal reality of Christ's saving grace, which is always and everywhere operative among men, is brought to its historically signified completion in the sight of the whole world, as a sacramental symbol of mankind's inner unity which is accomplished in the Second Adam.

Since Christ is "the light of nations", the precise aim of the Church is to make this light visible among all peoples. For the Church is related to Christ as "a kind of sacrament or as a sign and an instrument both of an intimate union with God and the unity of the whole human race. . . ."[28] It is in such terms as these that the Fathers of Vatican II wished "to unfold more fully to the faithful of the Church and to the whole world the Church's own inner nature and universal mission."[29] But this can only be done through obedience to the Lord's final command: "Go, therefore . . ." (Matt. 28:19). And so it is that missionary activity, among the peoples who have not yet been evangelized, is regarded as the "highest and most holy function of the Church", the "fundamental duty of the people of God", the clearest manifestation of the living Christian faith, and a dynamic sign of the Lord's coming now and at the end.[30]

[27] *Ibid.*
[28] *Lumen Gentium*, no. 1.
[29] *Ibid.*
[30] *Ad Gentes*, nos. 4-6, 9, 29, 35.

# VI

## Sacramental Symbolism

> One of the things I always forbid my
> students to say is "only a symbol".
> This bad phrase is rooted in the con-
> fusion of sign and symbol. Signs point
> to something different in which they
> do not participate at all. Symbols par-
> ticipate in the power of what they
> symbolize.
>
> PAUL TILLICH

A gesture, a movement of eyes, of a hand, a finger: these
are symbolic signs. They are meaningful ways of human
communication, proceeding intrinsically from what they
signify. A smile, a frown, a single tear: these contain much
more than merely verbal concepts, and they tell us immediately much more than might be communicated in a
whole essay. A sigh, a chuckle, as well as a spoken word:
these body forth symbolically the hidden mysteries of the
human person. The story behind them is not fully revealed,
yet it is contained in them vitally and significantly. Such
signs are shaped by their particular historical context; so
they are always incomplete, passing, conditional, and subject
to misinterpretation. The bodily conduct of a man, while
symbolizing all that he is, is not the whole man. He is always
much more than he appears to be, and in some ways he is
also much less.

Like all created things, including even the man Jesus who
speaks God's love to men, symbols stand for much more than
what they are manifestly in themselves. Through themselves

D                          97

they point beyond themselves to that in which they participate. What is conditional implies, and its own being proceeds from, what is unconditional. So tangible realities are more than what they seem to be; and "the more" is known to us only through "the less". Symbolism is thus the appropriate language of religion. This language alone, as Paul Tillich has said repeatedly, is able to express the ultimate.[1]

The whole world of grace, especially in so far as this world gives meaning to the Church, is to be understood, first of all then, in symbolic terms. The Christian vocation to the life of explicit faith within the visible structure of the Church is to be considered primarily in this language of sacramentality. Here we may see the fuller meaning of the Tridentine phrase, used in reference to the sacramental body of Christ: "a symbol of a sacred thing and the visible form of invisible grace".[2] Because the grace of Christ permeates the whole of redeemed humanity, the Church stands in symbolic representation as the universal sacrament of humanity united in Christ.

A symbol effects what it signifies, because it is the very thing which it represents and renders present significantly, although it is not co-extensively identical with the unconditional fullness of what it signifies. It is just enough of the reality itself, presented in the realm of spatio-temporal phenomenon, to be and to do what is signified. As a manifestation, bodying forth its own hidden reality, the symbol remains distinct from the whole reality which it represents, although the two are joined by an intrinsic, essential, causal relationship. This causality is mutual, with the initiative and priority belonging always to the signified reality.

We are of course speaking here only about natural,

[1] Cf. P. Tillich, *Dynamics of Faith* (Harper, New York, 1958), pp. 41 ff., and *Theology of Culture* (Oxford University Press, New York, 1964), pp. 53 ff.
[2] *Denzinger's Enchiridion Symbolorum*, 876.

universal and intrinsic symbols: those which arise from the very nature of things, not from mere conventions. A person is thus symbolized by his own living body. The action, growth and extension of the body *is* the person who acts, grows and extends himself, but not at once with the fullness of his self-manifestation. Since man on earth is bound to the consecutiveness of history, no single act of his in any moment of time can comprehensively signify all that he is. God alone comprehends the whole man at a glance, while the insights of men are always mediated through the limited acts of tangible bodies which are conditional and passing and ambiguously unfolding their inner meanings.

It is in this sense that Christ, who stands symbolically for the whole of humanity (the Second Adam), is at the same time the symbol of God. He is God in the consecutiveness of historical tangibility. He is God's historical self-revelation in human terms, because it is only in these terms that man can have any understanding of God. And this is why Christ as a tangible symbol in time, and thus also passing in time, is continued sacramentally in different times and places through the living symbolism of the Church whose actions are vivified by the same Holy Spirit who lives in Christ. So the Church, as the universal sacrament of Christ, effects what she signifies to the extent that she really makes Christ universally present in the mode of explicit and living significance among the nations in their own historical times and places.

The natural symbols of human love really contain and effectively communicate what they signify universally. The embrace of a mother and her child vivifies the inner mutual reality of love from which it proceeds, and which it expresses explicitly. Any communication within the human condition requires the intermediary of fleshy bodies, and symbolical language is more vital than any other. So God's self-communication to men always involves some measure of symbolic embodiment, or sacramentality.

The mutual self-donation symbolized in the gestures and in the consummation of conjugal love bring to an effective realization, with a certain historical tangibility and creative completion, the very love from which they proceed significantly and representatively. Humans may of course use these signs deceptively and hypocritically, but God's manifestations are always true, even though man's vision of the truths of revelation is always "obscure" and "partial" (I Cor. 13 : 12). And these very symbols of conjugal love are used repeatedly in Scripture to signify God's loving embrace of humanity in, and through, and on account of, His Incarnate Word's union with the Church: Christ stands for God's creative love and, at the same time, for the whole of His beloved creation. What God does symbolically is done in reality beyond our comprehension. "The great distinction," as Bouyer puts it, "between God's Word and man's word is that when God says something He also does it: He does it by the very fact that He says it."[3]

The symbolical language of religion is, in Reinhold Niebuhr's explanation, analogous to artistic communication: "Art describes the world not in terms of exact relationships. It constantly falsifies these relationships, as analysed by science, in order to express their total meaning."[4] In painting a portrait the artist falsifies the present mood and the actual appearance in order to embrace in one transcendent vision all of the moods and years that make a man what he is. Such a picture reflects the truth far more fully than a scientifically exact photograph which captures only one mood and literally identifies the whole man with only one

[3] *Life and Liturgy* by Louis Bouyer (Sheed & Ward, London, 1962), p. 105.
[4] *Beyond Tragedy* by Reinhold Niebuhr (Scribner's, New York, 1937), p. 3.

fleeting moment of his existence. Nor does the artist draw parallel lines exactly parallel. He puts them at angles in order to show depth, perspective, and a second dimension on the one-dimensional flat surface of his canvas. In various ways of provisional and superficial deception he strives to show us much more than is truly on the canvas when scientifically analysed.

In similar ways religious symbolism presents the eternal things of God in the dimension of time, revealing and expressing the eternal in temporal terms which contain, but far from exhaustively, what they signify. And this cannot be done without some measure of distortion for the sake of truth. As Niebuhr suggests, this paradox of religious communication in symbolical forms seems to be expressed in St Paul's famous description of the character, the vicissitudes and the faith of the Christian ministry: "as deceivers and yet truthful, as unknown and yet well known" (II Cor. 6:8).

The eternal Word creates, permeates and refashions the whole of creation from the beginning to the end of time. From creation itself the Word came forth into visible history, and now continues to manifest God's loving self-communication through the sacramental symbolism of the Church among the nations, in preparation for the full manifestation of His presence at the end. As the Father sends the Son, so the Son sends the Church, to all men. As Christ is the efficacious symbol of God's love in tangible history, so the Church is the sacrament of Christ among the nations who stand symbolically for mankind because they are mankind in the extension of historical time and place, and in the natural bonds of unity which men experience universally as social beings.

The symbolical force of the biblical "nations" is not rendered invalid by the fact that a minority of humanity, living in the Western world under the influence of the Industrial Revolution and the philosophies of individualism, has largely lost this sense of family unity and common destiny. Nor is this anthropological category here and now irrelevant to the majority of mankind merely because Western culture appears to be absorbing all "lesser cultures" into one new world dominated by the economics of technology. Theology is not based on sociological conjecture concerning the future. The Romans thought they had unified the nations too. But God, who separated the families of men, has His own way of "making a great people, all one" —without any man-made Tower of Babel.

Because of the obvious biological, cultural and historical continuity which makes a people one (in their own estimation and in the judgment of their neighbours), the "tribes and tongues and peoples and nations" are still the universally relevant, natural and appropriate symbols through which the Church, by establishing herself among them on firm and indigenous foundations, takes on the flesh required for the prolongation and concrete universalization of God's saving Word in history. The nations are to the sacramental self-realization of the Church what human bodies are to the sacrament of matrimony. It is only in terms of his own biological and social community of origin and experience that any man may have an awareness of his corporate destiny and his solidarity with the whole of humanity.

So the universal mission of the new messianic people of God is one of sacramental (symbolical) representation, mediation and intercession—always of course in faithful union with the Incarnate Word on account of whom, and through whom, the whole body of redeemed humanity (summed up symbolically in the Church) is presented with new life. It is a matter of doing sacramentally among each people (in the consecutiveness of history) what the eternal

Word does actually among all men (in the ever present *now* of all history), and what Christ has done "once and for all" among one people (within the limits of a particular historical time and place).

There are also countless conventional symbols through which this mystery has been expressed. Thus, Father Congar:

> Each of us in his own little world, all of us for the world at large—we are Jacob's ladder. The representative going up of mankind to God and the representative coming down of Jesus Christ to the world pass through us. The whole Church is sacramental and missionary, and so is each Christian in his degree. Each member of any group (e.g. a parish, *family*, *tribe*, *people*, *nation*) that seeks Christ through the Church stands for the whole group. To what extent do they effectively aid the whole group in its journey to God? It cannot be known. But they are the first fruits, a sheaf offered up, and they are intercessors for it: had there been ten righteous men in the city, God would have spared it (Gen. 18:32).[5]

The "first fruits" are not the only fruits of God's universally salvific will. They are the part standing, in terms of "corporate personality", for all the others.[6] These others grow abundantly both before and after a "sheaf" is offered up from them, and for them, representatively. The Church, as the sacramental continuation of the Incarnation, stands for God's gift of Himself to all of humanity, and for all of His un-named people who, scattered as they are among the nations from the beginning to the end of history, respond internally to His offer and return to Him only through the hidden operations of grace. But a visible *remnant* of them is returning tangibly, after the representative manner of "first fruits", in the name of all the others—in

---

[5] *The Wide World My Parish*, p. 21; words added in italics.
[6] Cf. previous chapter, pp. 88 ff.

the name of Christ who stands for all. This is the Church among the nations: a gathering of men among other gatherings of men, the company of Christ's witnesses in the world.

The present meaning and efficacy of this sacramental community among men is derived intrinsically from God's continuously saving work within creation, but always with explicit reference to the historical advent of the Word in human flesh and to His coming at the end of history. So the Church, within her own appropriate realm of sacramentality, does not do less than what Christ has done "once and for all". Any sacramental enactment signifies therefore, in the very first place, God's offer of saving grace to the whole of humanity. It signifies the actual conferral and acceptance of grace among men, *"propter nos homines"*, even when the immediate participant in the sacramental action may himself be closed through sin to the grace which is there and then offered under a visible sign and pledge of God's invisible mercy.

Any notion of sacramental causality, in so far as it ignores the meaning of symbolism, tends to promote the practice of magic. To think of the dynamics of the Church in purely literalistic and non-symbolical categories leads, moreover, to intolerance and to pharisaism. It is quite wrong to consider the sacraments only as instrumental sources of grace, or simply as causes of grace, for the Christians who participate in them. This leads directly to the "mistaken idea that the sacraments afford an easy way to salvation, or that they demand nothing more than that one does not place an obstacle to their innate efficacy."[7] The presuppositions for a fruitful reception of the sacraments are not merely negative, nor is sacramental grace produced automatically, as many Catholics have come to believe through

[7] Denis O'Callaghan, "Introduction", *Sacraments: The Gestures of Christ*, Ed. D. O'Callaghan (Sheed & Ward, New York, 1964), p. xi.

a misunderstanding of the philosophical expression *"ex opere operato"*.[8]

The sacraments are a public manifestation of the faith of the Church: they are "the sacraments of faith".[9] So they presuppose, in those who approach them, an authentic Christian faith and a genuine obedience to the mission of the Church. Indeed, they presuppose the presence of grace which alone moves men towards God. The liturgy of the Church, which embraces all of the sacraments, is thus "the outstanding means" of nourishing the faith and hope and love which Christians require for their primary function of proclaiming Christ to all men.[10] "The liturgy thereby reveals the Church as a sign raised up among the nations (Isa. 11:12); and under this sign the scattered sons of God are being gathered into one . . . (John 11:52).[11]

The production of sacramental grace should not therefore be regarded simply in the terms of cause and effect, without reference to the universal mission of the Church as the fundamental reason for the existence of the sacraments. According to Otto Semmelroth, "the magisterium of the Church, especially the Council of Trent, prefers to express the salvific meaning of the sacraments in the words, they confer grace (*conferunt*), or contain it (*continent*)."[12] This way of looking at it should help us to avoid the "cause-effect automatism" (or practical magic) so characteristic of the Nominalistic sacramental theology of the recent past.[13]

The elementary point to keep in mind during any dis-

---

[8] For a detailed discussion of this whole matter, with all the appropriate references, see Piet Fransen, in *Christian Revelation and World Religions*, pp. 70 ff.

[9] Cf. *Sacrosanctum Concilium*, no. 59.

[10] *Ibid.*, nos. 2, 6, 10, 59.

[11] *Ibid.*, no. 2.

[12] *Church and Sacrament* by Otto Semmelroth, s.j. (Gill, Dublin, 1965), p. 93.

[13] Cf. Fransen, *loc. cit.*

cussion of the sacraments is that they belong to the category of signs, as St Thomas Aquinas demonstrated a long time ago;[14] so their causality must belong to the mode of signification. Trent also said that baptism is an "instrumental cause" of the "grace of justification". But this is to be understood only against the clearly stated background in which all of the sacraments are seen as imparting "that kind of grace which is represented by sign and symbol", as Semmelroth has shown. "The sacrament," he continues, "is a sign in as much as it presents to man's mind a symbolic representation of invisible grace, so that he can decide for or against it."[15]

The universal aspect of the sacraments must also be stressed far more than it has been in the recent past. It is a matter of considerable importance for Christians to appreciate that, according to an earlier and more authentic tradition than that of our nineteenth-century manuals of theology, the Church's diverse ritual actions, known as the seven sacraments, are what they are precisely because the Church herself is the sacrament of Christ.[16] It is not because of these seven basic forms of her self-expression that the Church is sacramental. It is just the other way around. These actions are sacramental because of what the Church is in the very first place: *The universal sacrament of mankind's salvation.*[17] So the prior significance of any sacramental action is that, through Christ, the grace of reconciliation is offered to the whole of humanity. Indeed, on account of the universal efficacy of Christ's love for all sinners, this grace is actually conferred on men, even though it is done "for the most part anonymously", anywhere and at

[14] *Summa Theol.*, III, q. 60, a. 1; cf. Semmelroth, *op. cit.*, p. 94.
[15] *Op. cit.*, p. 94.
[16] Cf. "Christ, Sacrament of God" by Denis O'Callaghan, and "Acts of Christ: Signs of Faith" by Cornelius Ernst, O.P., in *Sacraments: The Gestures of Christ*, pp. 25, 73.
[17] Cf. *Lumen Gentium*, nos. 1, 9, 48.

any time, with or without immediately visible signs.[18]

From this it follows that the sacraments have saving significance for Christians who participate in them, primarily because these Christians are members of humanity whose salvation is signified primordially by the historical existence of the Church. In these actions the chosen people, standing symbolically with Christ for the whole of humanity, are exercising their highest representative function; and through this obedience to their special vocation they are themselves the visibly blessed "first fruits" of redemption, the living sign of saving grace among the nations, and the tangible fulfilment (in actual history among the nations) of the promise made to Abraham.

What Christians do in the Church is not primarily for themselves, and then only secondarily for the whole world. It is, again, just the other way around. As Christ came to give Himself for others, to be sanctified and consecrated for them (John 17:19), so also the members of the Church are called primarily for all the others to whom they are sent as witnesses. Only through their actual obedience to this vocation are Christians themselves sanctified by what they manifest in the sacramental actions of the Church. Among Christians, liturgy and life must go hand in hand.

"God does not make men holy and save them merely as individuals, without bond or link between one another."[19] Whether or not each one is explicitly aware of it, He sanctifies them as members of His whole redeemed people through Christ who is the Head of this new family of Adam. So there is nothing narrowly individualistic and "self-saving" in liturgical piety. The immediate participants in the sacramental life of the Church are, by reason of their historical vocation through explicit faith, the representatives of

[18] Cf. chapters two and three, above.
[19] *Lumen Gentium*, no. 9.

redeemed humanity. They are the living sign of every man's constant need, and his present possibility, of accepting the grace of saving sanctification which is always and everywhere offered to all, and without which no man has even a hope of attaining the end for which he was made. And all of this is so, on account of Christ who, through the extension of His Church among the nations, continues to prepare the world for His final coming when all things shall have been historically completed, sacramentally summed up and recapitulated, in the "fullness of Him who is wholly fulfilled in all" (Eph. 1:23).

The sacramental significance of the Church may be fully achieved among a particular people, even though the Church may not be juridically and numerically co-extensive with every single member of this people. As Christ stands for all mankind, so the Church, firmly and indigenously established among a particular people, stands for all men of that nation. Still it is normally expected, assuming proper pastoral care, that the existing flock in each nation should "grow stronger in the faith and increase in numbers daily" (Acts 16:5). What matters most, however, is not the numbers of individual Christians found in one or another particular place. Certainly there must be enough of them to sustain the normal life of the Church among their own people precisely in order that they might be able to make their contribution to the extension of the Church among the other peoples who have not yet known Christ sacramentally.

Again, precisely because of the Church's symbolic nature, the completion of her mission of self-incarnation among the nations, who stand symbolically for the whole of mankind, should not be taken in a numerically and quantitatively inclusive sense. In the course of history some peoples cease to exist as distinctive ethnic-culture units, and new peoples come into being, for various sociological reasons.

The point is that the Church must be raised up among enough of the peoples to symbolize adequately the real presence of Christ among all men in every part of the world. Nor should we imagine that this sacramental presence of the Church will be, at some future date, realized concretely throughout the whole world *contemporaneously*, and seen by all men at once. "All men" do not exist in history contemporaneously. The process of redemptive history unfolds, and leads to its final goal, only *consecutively*; and the Church on earth is herself subject to this very temporal condition of humanity.

# VII

## The Christian Vocation

> Election is always at bottom election for others.
>
> JOSEPH RATZINGER

Missionaries have many occasions to observe—and they have often remarked on this—that the human conduct of Christians is not manifestly superior to that of non-Christians, according to the lights which are available to them within their respective historical situations. Those who belong visibly to the Church do not generally appear to be better people, or holier, than those on the "outside". All men are sinners (Rom. 3:23; 7:23; I John 1:8). "None is righteous, no, not one" (Rom. 3:10). Even one of the first to have been chosen by the Lord Himself was later called a "son of perdition" (John 17:12). Do those therefore on the "inside" really respond to grace "more easily" or "more frequently" than "the rest of men"?

Even our common historical experience suggests a negative reply; and this may be confirmed by a little introspection. To imagine the opposite is, however, a special temptation of Christians. It is a temptation to the sin of self-righteousness: the sin of those who fall precisely because they are so sure that they are standing. Is this not the sin against the Holy Spirit: the sin that renders men morally incapable of repentance? One cannot repent if he does not recognize his need for repentance.

Here is the supreme irony of the Christian vocation. It is a matter of giving witness, in a sinful world, to the reality of saving sanctification. Christians are called to share explicitly in the very perfection of their heavenly Father. They must proclaim this before men. Yet they dare not try to measure the achievement. For he who considers himself more upright than the rest of men, or even accounts himself capable of achieving greater goodness and sanctity, is already wading precariously in the swamp of pharisaism. Still, this posture of the righteous-elect is quite as common among believers today as it was among the "chosen people" in the time of Christ and in the days of Isaiah. It is still just as "inane" as the prophet described it. The Christian is nothing, if he is not first of all a "publican". This is the only authentic starting point for any re-examination of the Christian vocation.

With good historical sense, as well as theological acumen, the Council Fathers of Vatican II recognized this officially when they spoke of the Church as a community of saints and sinners at the same time : *"sancta simul et purificanda"*.[1] The phrase is humbly reminiscent of Luther's *"justus simul et peccator"*;[2] and it signifies the authentic attitude of Christianity before the rest of the world which is also made up of "sinners, at the same time holy and always in need of being purified".[3]

In his existential situation every man is a member of redeemed humanity, but no one has absolute certitude about his own final salvation or that of his brother. Each is always in need of God's mercy, since each one really is a sinner who constantly sins. Because of the abounding power of Christ's victorious grace, sin can be avoided, although no man has any certain guarantee that he will in fact avoid it.

[1] *Lumen Gentium*, no. 8.
[2] For the Catholic understanding of this paradox, see : *Theological Dictionary* by K. Rahner and H. Vorgrimler (Burns & Oates, London, Herder & Herder, New York, 1965), p. 435.
[3] *Lumen Gentium*, no. 8.

So the condition of "fear and trembling" is the same for all; and he to whom more is given, whether he belongs visibly to the Church or not, incurs the greater risk.

The pharisaical attitude, which is often so subtly expressed that it is not recognized by its real name, follows from the erroneous belief that men are called to visible membership in the Church primarily for their own comfort, consolation, and salvation; and that the reception of the sacraments, which are "for them", is bound automatically to provide them with "more grace" (and thus greater holiness and moral uprightness) than the others for whom the sacraments are not immediately available. Christians, as the argument goes, have the "ordinary" means of salvation, while most of humanity has "only" some vague "extraordinary" means. The tacit assumption is that the word "extraordinary" in this context means somehow "less effective" or "less assured", instead of "not yet completed historically". The suggestion is that there are two *really* different ways of salvation, instead of the one and only way of being "related" to Christ through grace (which is always and only sacramental), and thus "belonging" to Christ at least through implicit faith.

Against this self-soothing conception there stands the whole biblical teaching about vocation: it always means election for something outside of one's self, and it always involves risk. Christians are not chosen primarily for their own salvation but for God's service, or ministry, in and for the whole world. This call is not a vocation to a state of privileged favouritism. It is first and foremost an assignment in history to "a post of responsibility for service", as Congar expressed it.[4] The "devout" Christian who has found "safety

---

[4] "The Church: The People of God" by Yves Congar, O.P., *Concilium*, vol. 1, no. 1 (Jan. 1965), pp. 8, 10; see also *The Theology of Vocations* by C. A. Schleck, C.S.C. (Bruce, Milwaukee, 1963), pp. 6-7, 9-10, 13-14, 16-17.

and security" in the Church, without having to risk anything that he has or is, and without having to die daily to
himself, is one who has abandoned his vocation: sold out
for a mess of pottage. It is important for every Christian
to be devout—"provided," as Barth says, "that devotion
means obedience to the call, Follow *me*, which may perhaps
lead us away from everything that the conservative or the
liberal calls devotion."[5] The Christian is one who is elected
to represent others by serving God's revealed purpose, at
whatever personal cost, in the *real* world.

The Lord's gesture of washing the feet of the Apostles
(John 13:1-20) dramatized the meaning of the word *diakonos*
which He used to characterize His position in the world and
that of His followers (Luke 22:27; Matt. 20:26-28). In
English we translate this as "minister" or "servant", but the
New Testament connotation is "lackey" or "slave"; and in
the writing of St Paul *diakonos* is used on a parallel with
*doulos* which has the literal denotation of "slave".[6] So the
followers of Christ are not chosen for themselves primarily
but for the service of others.

Since God decided to save the world in an incarnational
way, He uses human instruments. And weak instruments
they are, who may take no credit to themselves, as the mercy
of God is made manifest in the world through their lives
among the nations: through their faith and hope and love.
Since men are social beings, they are not sanctified and
saved merely as individuals but as members of a people,[7]
for whom they are given "varied functions" in order to

[5] *The Word of God and The Word of Man* by Karl Barth, trans. by
D. Horton (Harper, New York, 1957), p. 131.
[6] Cf. *Human Achievement and Divine Vocation in the Message of Paul*
by W. A. Beardslee (SCM Press, London, 1961), pp. 95 ff.; *Authority in the
Church* by John L. McKenzie, s.j. (Geoffrey Chapman, London, Sheed
& Ward, New York, 1966), p. 23.
[7] *Lumen Gentium*, no. 9.

build up the frame of Christ's body (Eph. 4:11-16) in the extension of different historical times and places.[8]

The historically chosen people of Israel is a type for our understanding of the vocation of this new and sacramentally messianic people of the final days:[9] "Now these things happened to them as a warning . . . for our instruction, upon whom the end of ages has come. Therefore let anyone who thinks that he stands take heed lest he fall" (I Cor. 10: 11-12). The lesson was stated succinctly by Douglas Webster: "Across the end of the Old Testament story might be written these words: Mission Abandoned."[10] Now what about the obedience of the new Israel who are chosen also for a mission? Their prior mission is to become, through their commitment to the "highest and most holy function of the Church",[11] a light of revelation among all peoples.

The original people of Israel were not chosen for their "surpassing numbers" nor for their worldly power and significance. They were the "fewest of any people" (Deut. 7: 7), and the most despised of their contemporaries. From all accounts they seem to have been a particularly intractable lot: a "rebel brood", economically "naked" and culturally "unwashed" (Ezek. 16:3-14). As such they were an appropriate symbol of humanity and an apt instrument for the manifestation through them of God's power; so He made them into *a people* for the world to stumble over and to reckon with. But only a handful of them, "a faithful remnant" (a progressively diminishing segment of mankind), was finally available for God's purpose of making present

[8] *Ibid.*, n. 18.
[9] Cf. *Mary, Mother of the Redemption* by E. Schillebeeckx (Sheed & Ward, London, 1964), pp. 153 ff.
[10] *Local Church and World Mission* by D. Webster (SCM Press, London, 1962), p. 61.
[11] *Ad Gentes*, no. 29.

in actual history His light of revelation for the nations.

It is not surprising therefore that, in forming His new people into an external sociological entity called the Church, the Lord was not at all concerned with gathering great numbers of followers in one particular nation, His very own nation. Instead, He devoted His missionary life to the task of gathering a "small flock" from among the members of this one particular ethnic-culture unit of men. As the Lord Himself was sent for others, so His new people were called into existence for the sake of others. He formed them as missionaries to be sent to *other peoples*. Their own salvation, and the wide acceptance of Christ among their own people, became conditional in relation to their obedience in this matter of going forth to the very ends of the earth.

This dynamic meaning of the Church was fully dramatized in the events of Pentecost and in the lives of the Apostles who actually went out to other peoples in order to establish among them this very same missionary community. Through this constant "fanning out" of the missionary Church the ends of the earth would eventually be reached and all of the nations would eventually come to hear the good news of their salvation in Christ. The universal aims of Christianity are always prior. A Christian community's growth and vitality among its own particular people is proportionately related to its missionary commitments among the other peoples who have not yet known Christ in His sacramental sign of salvation raised up among them on firm and indigenous foundations.

As the symbolic representative of God's concern for humanity, Israel of old was chosen for the explicit service of God's purpose in history: chosen to stand, in tangible history, for the whole of mankind. Individuals within the chosen group were given particular vocations through

which they contributed concretely towards the final historical realization of the one mission of the whole group:
Abraham, for example, Joseph, Jeremiah, the Virgin Mary,
John the Baptist, and so many others both named and un-
named. The accounts of their deeds show that election in
Scripture is always for some task to be accomplished in
history. Vocation is always in the first place a matter of
being sent in order to accomplish something outside of one's
self, and the mission usually involves far more personal
inconvenience and risk than comfort and security. The story
of Jonah is highly instructive in this connection. The disobedience of this missionary brought him and all of his
fellow travellers to the verge of total personal ruination.
Even the final success of his reluctantly accomplished mission left him a broken man, confirmed in the futility of his
own efforts and convinced that he should have remained
in his own country.

In his remarkably comprehensive and eloquent treatment
of the Christian notion of election, Karl Barth seeks to
resolve in a grand synthesis the dialectical antithesis of the
elected and the rejected: the few who are chosen and the
many who are not, Israel and the nations. The reconciliation takes place primarily and properly in Christ who is the
One chosen by God for the sake of all. "If we would know,"
writes Barth, "what it was that God elected for Himself
when He elected fellowship with man, then we can answer
only that He elected our rejection. He made it His own. He
bore it and suffered it with all its most bitter consequences.
For the sake of this choice and for the sake of man He
hazarded Himself wholly and utterly. He elected our suffering (what we as sinners must suffer towards Him and before
Him and from Him). He elected it as His own suffering. This
is the extent to which His election is an election of grace,
an election of love, an election to give Himself, an election

to empty and abase Himself for the sake of the elect. . . . That is how God loved the world."[12]

But those who are chosen from among men were first among the rejected. So Christ's own election is fundamentally for the sake of the rejected: for those who are not chosen. In this sense Christ is "*the* Rejected, as and because He is *the* Elect".[13] "In view of His election," Barth continues, "there is no other rejected but Himself. It is just for the sake of the election of all the rejected that He stands in solitude over against them all. It is just for them that He is *the* rejected One (in His rejection making room for them as the elect of God). . . ."[14] Christ does not therefore exist for Himself or for the sake of Himself, "but as the reality and the revelation of the will of God on behalf of an unlimited number of other men."[15] The basis of Barth's synthesis may perhaps be summarized in the following four sentences on the election of Christ, *the* chosen One:

> He is elected as the reality and the revelation of the omnipotent loving-kindness of God towards these many. He is elected to bear their rejection, but also to overcome and therefore to complete in Himself their own eternal election in time. He is elected, therefore, to be for them the promise and proclamation of their own election. Jesus Christ is, therefore, what He is—the Elect—for these many.[16]

All of this applies secondarily—in the realm of sacramental symbolism and explicit faith—to those who have been chosen to follow Christ in different historical times and places among the nations: the historical witnesses to the meaning of His election for the sake of all men. Hence the profoundly intrinsic and mutual relationship between the

---

[12] *Church Dogmatics*, II-2, pp. 164 ff.
[13] *Ibid.*, p. 353.
[14] *Ibid.*
[15] *Ibid.*, p. 421.
[16] *Ibid.*

Church and the rest of mankind: the few are chosen for the sake of the many, the few in whose faithful activity the convergence between general and special sacred history is being progressively symbolized in the extension of different historical times and places.[17] The explicit people of God are truly themselves only to the extent that they permit themselves to be used as a part of God's dealings with the *oikumene*; for the Church exists, and may be defined, simply as a functional participation in Christ's mission to the nations.[18] Where there is no functioning concern for this universal mission, there is no Church. Obedience to the Christian vocation must always be seen, therefore, in relation to the "ministry of reconciliation" (II Cor. 5:18), as the ministry is (or is not) being accomplished concretely in the real world.

This ministry, and nothing else, is the concrete determination under which the Christian vocation is lived; and this is so, precisely because of what Christ is: the reality and the reconciliation of the world rejected by God because of its sins. Aside from this, Christianity has no meaning, no relevance for the world. Aside from this, the Church signifies no more than is signified by the existence of any other tribal religion. It is in these terms that Barth explains the meaning of Christ's "little flock":

> If we ask about the meaning and the direction and the life of the elect . . . in the light of the person of Jesus Christ, we have to reply that the elect lives as such in so far as he is there on behalf of others, i.e., in so far as it is grounded in him and happens through him that the omnipotent loving-

[17] Cf. above, pp. 73 f.
[18] Cf. *The Church Inside Out* by J. C. Hoekendijk (SCM Press, London, 1964), p. 40: "Whatever else can be said about the church may be of only little relevance. The *nature* of the church can be sufficiently defined by its *function*. . . . To proclaim the gospel of the Kingdom throughout the oikoumene is the church's *opus proprium*. . . ."

kindness of God is at all events directed and opened up to the world, i.e., to others among those who do not yet recognize it and are not yet grateful for it.[19]

So what is predicated of Christ, who is among other things the "expected of the nations", may also be predicated of the Church: of all who have been chosen for the life of explicit Christian faith. Their special vocation in history is portrayed exactly in the calling, appointment and mission of the Apostles. The commission to the twelve is given through them to the whole Church.[20] Once again in the words of Barth: "What it means to be in the Church, and even what the Church itself truly is, may be seen typically in what is described in the New Testament as the reality of the apostolate, and particularly in what Paul describes as the reality of his apostolate."[21]

The Christian vocation is therefore a commission to participate actively, according to one's station in life and one's ability, in the apostolic mission of the Church to the nations, i.e., to the peoples who have "not yet" known Christ in His Church among them on firm and indigenous foundations. The very word "apostle", first used by the Lord Himself to designate the twelve (and consequently the collegial body of their successors), is borrowed from Hebrew legal terminology where this word "*shaliah*" means one who is sent abroad to function as a legal agent of the sender whose authority he represents and in whose name he acts. The implication of "sending" or being "sent" abroad to other peoples, leaving one's own people and place of origin, is essential to the Christian notion of apostleship, which is a dynamic participation in the messianic mission of the Son of God: "As the Father sent me, so I send you" (John 20:21). It is for this

[19] *Church Dogmatics*, II-2, p. 423.
[20] *Ibid.*, pp. 427 ff.
[21] *Ibid.*, p. 430.

mission that grace is given to those who are called to visible membership in the Church. Mission and grace always go together in the Church. "Grace and apostleship" are given as one, "in order to bring about the obedience of faith for the sake of His name among the nations" (Rom. 1:5; 15:18; Acts 26:16-18; Gal. 2:7, 9).

By faithfully striving to do just this, in obedience to the final command of the Lord (Matt. 28:19), the members of the Church justify their own existence and attain hope in the real possibility of their own salvation. The hope of Christians is inseparable from their task of making known "among the nations" the previously "hidden mystery" of salvation, the "hope of glory" for all men (Col. 1:26-27). The Church exists for nothing less than this, and salvation "within" the Church is attained through nothing less than this obedience. In speaking of the typical Christian vocation of Mary, Father Rahner expressed the unity of grace and vocation in these words:

> A human being, endowed with grace, accepts grace in and through that grace, both for himself and for others, so that the acceptance which is personal for himself implies salvation for others, and the acceptance which is a co-operation in the salvation of others is precisely that act in which the grace of God is accepted for himself; in which the service which is one's own office, and one's own sanctification, simply become one and the same.[22]

So it is that the new people of God "are chosen in order that" they may "proclaim the perfections of Him" who called them "out of darkness" (I Peter 2:9). This is why the Church exists as a "priestly people", acting on behalf of all the others, as the sacramental instrument of mankind's sal-

[22] *Mission and Grace*, vol. I, p. 180; see also Karl Barth, *Church Dogmatics*, II-2, pp. 416 f., 431 f., 444; and *The Dynamic Element in the Church* by K. Rahner, p. 55.

vation. And they themselves, the Christians, are a "holy people" in order that they may serve, and only in so far as they actually serve, to raise up this universal sign of salvation among one new people after another. For each member of the Church, therefore—for each one according to his historical position and his particular function within the visible body of Christ—these words of St Paul become an ultimate vocational norm:

> Of that Gospel I was made a minister by the gift of God's grace. . . . Yes, to me, the very least of all the saints, there was given this grace, to announce among the nations the good tidings . . . and to enlighten all men as to what is the dispensation of the mystery which has been hidden from eternity in God . . . in order that the manifold wisdom of God might be made known through the Church . . . (Eph. 3: 7-11).

> Now I rejoice in my sufferings . . . and in my flesh I complete what is lacking in Christ's afflictions for the sake of his body, that is, the Church, of which I became a minister according to the divine office which was given to me for delivering God's message to you, the mystery hidden for ages and generations, but now made manifest to his saints. It was God's purpose to reveal it to them and to show among the nations all the rich glory of this mystery. The mystery is Christ among you, your hope of glory: this is the Christ we proclaim. . . . For this I struggle wearily on . . . (Col. 1:24-29).

As the Lord suffered in order to plant His Church on earth, so His followers must participate in His sufferings, as they go out of themselves for the sake of completing the frame of Christ's body in different times and places among the peoples who constitute mankind. If priority is given to this mission among the nations, if the members of the

Church die to themselves and to their own peoples in this way, then will the life of the whole Church be renewed, extended and deepened. There is no other way for Christians who believe that death in many forms is the price to be paid for the renewal of life. At the same time, any Christian community which is exclusively or even primarily turned inward upon itself signifies only its own death without renewal, because this is a death suffered for the sake of itself, not for the others.

The Lord comes to and for the whole of humanity through the hidden operations of grace; but He comes to Christians also through explicit faith which is given to them as the representatives of all the others. So the believer's desire for the coming of the Lord is at once personal, historical, universal, and eschatological. And this desire is the dynamic element in the Christian vocation; and it is the keenest incentive to missionary activity : "Come, Lord Jesus. . . . Thy Kingdom Come!" The authentic juridical members of the Church are "those who love His coming" (II Tim. 4:8), and who therefore do something about it positively in the here and now of history. For the Lord comes to Christians, or is present to them, only to the extent that they are striving to make Him present among all others.

The "hope" of the Christian vocation (Eph. 1:18; 4:4; Col. 1:27), and therefore the prior reason for the existence of the visible Church anywhere at any time, is this coming of Christ to all nations through the sacramentality of the Church, in preparation for His final and full presence to the whole of creation at the end of history. In his fifth *Sermon for Advent*, St Bernard reminds us that the sacramental coming of the Lord to the nations is the means whereby the world passes from His first historical advent to His final coming in glory. As the first advent was accomplished through the historical "remnant" of God's people in the flesh of Israel, so the final coming is now being progressively achieved through the sacramental "remnant" of His new people in the flesh of every tribe and tongue and people and nation. It is *from them* that the body of His new eschatological Israel is being made up in this last age of salvation history. It is *through them* that the Church is becoming universal in history and the cultural "riches of the nations" are flowing into the new Zion, thus fulfilling and expressing the catholic nature of the Church.

So it is that missionary activity is the specific and primary function through which the Church progressively accomplishes her mission to the world, in the consecutive terms of history, and thus "hastens towards the day" of His coming (II Peter 3:11-12). For this sign of salvation, which is the Church, must *first* be raised up among the nations, and then shall the end come (Mark 13:10; Matt. 24:14).[23] It is a matter of building up the temple which "the glory of God lights up", so that "the nations may walk by the light thereof" (Apoc. 21:23-24). It is a matter of "planting the Church" everywhere in one new field after another, so that the seed of unity, hope and salvation may take root and bud forth among all peoples, and thus grow into the universally visible tree of life—"for the healing of the nations" (Apoc. 22:2).

Such is the meaning of Father Ratzinger's sentence with which we introduced this chapter: "Election is always at bottom election for others." At the same time we have also seen the meaning of his very next sentence in the same context: "For the Church, as for the individual, election is identical with the missionary obligation."[24]

---

[23] Cf. *Ad Gentes*, no. 9.
[24] *Christian Brotherhood* by Joseph Ratzinger (Sheed & Ward, London, 1966), p. 80.

# VIII

## The Prior Mission of the Church

> It is time the missionary encounter
> were set firmly at the centre of our
> theological concern.
>
> AREND TH. VAN LEEUWEN

The Church is not sent to save the world through a
juridical encounter with as many people as possible (or
convenient) anywhere and everywhere simultaneously, so
that an ever increasing number of men may, by joining
the Church, be given "better means" of salvation, with the
hope that their holiness and goodness will somehow radiate
out from them to the rest of humanity, and thus progressively transform the world into a suitable place for the
Lord's eventual return. The same sanctification is already
offered authentically to all men. The world will never be
"more saved" than it is right now. For Jesus *is* the Lord of
all. The transformation, or reconciliation, of the world is not
a mathematically cumulative and humanly measurable process. It is something that is already taking place always
and everywhere among men through the universally operative and victorious grace of Christ, even though this may
be recognized only by the eyes of faith. Exactly in what,
then, does the mission of the Church consist?

The Church is sent as a witness, to announce in words,
to proclaim by deeds, and thus to communicate sacramentally to the whole world the good news of Christian revelation; the hopeful and astonishing news that, in spite of all
appearances, men do not die and the world is not lost; and

this, on account of One Man's obedience to His historical mission.[1] The communication of this message to mankind is to be accomplished through the obedience of Christians, dying daily to themselves in union with their Lord, and bearing all the marks of His worldly failure, for the sake of their eschatological mission to the nations. "To go out preaching at His command", the Lord called "those whom it pleased Him to call" (Mark 3:13-14). This, above all else, is what is meant by the Christian's vocation to co-operate in the redemption of the world.

There has been much well-intentioned confusion on the subject in recent years. So, some further theological precision is called for. If the Pentecostal mission of the Church is supposed to become significantly the reversal of Babel, then the aim of this sending must first be seen clearly; and an order of priorities in the organization of the Church's energies, and in the distribution of her resources, must be recognized unequivocally in relation to the aim.

The very first line of the decree of Vatican II on missionary activity tells us that the Church is sent "to the nations" as the "all-embracing sacrament of salvation". As the vocation of God's historically chosen people of Israel is intelligible only in reference to the nations of the earth, so the meaning of His new and eschatological people may be found and realized only in relation to these ethnic-culture units of men who constitute the *oikumene*, for and from whom the Church exists. This aspect is given pre-eminence also, as we

---

[1] According to Bernard Cooke, s.j., "Christianity has a unique perspective to communicate to man, a unique and paradoxical insight into the structure of human existence and human meaning. The basic truth of Christianity, around which everything else turns, is the mystery of the death and resurrection of Christ. This is the Gospel; this is the first kerygma which formed the Christian community itself, and on the basis of which it approached the world. . . ." Cf. "Existential Pertinence of Religion" by B. Cooke, *Concilium*, vol. 9, no. 2 (Nov. 1966), p. 17, British edition.

have seen, in the *Constitution on the Church*: *Lumen Gentium*. This "light to the nations" exists for the precise purpose of bringing salvation to all men, *sacramentally*. For the Church is the symbolic instrument and the efficacious pledge, to be planted as a seed among all peoples, through which God's promise to Abraham shall be tangibly fulfilled before the end: "All together in you shall the nations of the earth be blessed" (Gen. 12:3).

Such is God's "ecumenical purpose" in history: protology and eschatology meet in missionary activity directed to the peoples who have not yet heard the good news of their salvation in Christ.[2] The Pentecostal sending, initiating the Church on earth, signifies the end (Acts 2:17; I Peter 4:7), while actually leading the world to its final day (Mark 13:10; Matt. 24:14). So missionary work as such is the specific function through which the Church seeks to achieve the goal that was set for her on Pentecost. This is why it is called "the highest and most holy function of the Church".[3] From this all of the "varied ministries" (I Cor. 12:4) and the different "functions" (Rom. 12:4) derive their first meaning and their final justification in the service of the Church's one mission of building up the body of Christ throughout the world (Eph. 4:12).

If missionary work[4] is thus the prior function through which the Church strives directly, systematically, and progressively to serve her primary reason for existing, then

[2] Cf. "The Mission of the People of God" by Johannes Blauw, *The Missionary Church in East and West*, Edited by C. C. West and D. M. Paton (SCM Press, London, 1959), pp. 91 ff.

[3] *Ad Gentes*, no. 29.

[4] For the precise notion of missionary activity, see chapter one, footnote 12; and notice that, in the Decree *Ad Gentes*, missionary evangelization is functionally identified with "planting the Church" where it has not been before. See also Cardinal Agagianian's "Address at Burgos", August 10, 1966, in *Christ to the World*, vol. XII, no. I (1967), p. 19: "The primary object of the general mission of the Church is precisely missionary activity in the strict sense. . . ."

every other activity of the Church must come after this, both in the order of time and of urgency. Hence, all of the Church's pastoral and social works on behalf of her present members, as well as efforts directed towards Christian reunion, are meaningful and justified in so far as they are subordinated to the final missionary orientation of the whole Church, and in so far as they involve some positive contribution to the task of announcing the Gospel to the remaining peoples who have not yet seen the sign of their salvation raised up among them on firm and indigenous foundations. Without this catholic orientation, the various activities of the Church, good and interesting as they may be in themselves, are simply outside of the Christian frame of reference.

In order to reach a better understanding of this utterly basic point, some additional ground-clearing still seems necessary.[5] In the very first place, "we must rid ourselves once and for all", as Professor van Leeuwen expresses it, "of the idea that somehow or other Western civilization has got to be or can be 're-Christianized' through some restoration, in a new guise, of the *Corpus Christianum*." At least we ought to stop thinking and acting as though this problem of the "de-Christianized masses" in parts of Europe and the Americas should now become the major concern of those who have been called for the specifically missionary ministry of the Church. "To put it bluntly," in the words of J. C. Hoekendijk, "the call to evangelism is often little else than a call to restore 'Christendom'. . . as a solid, well-integrated cultural complex, directed and dominated by the Church. And the sense of urgency is often nothing but a nervous feel-

---

[5] For more of this ground-clearing, see Hillman, *op. cit.*, especially Chapters I and II; and "The Main Task of the Mission", in *Concilium*, vol. 3, no. 2 (March 1966), pp. 3 ff., British edition.

[6] *Christianity in World History*, p. 410.

ing of insecurity, with the established church endangered; a flurried activity to save the remnants of a time now irrevocably past."[7]

The grace of Christ is not now less available to the peoples of the Western world than it was during the hey-day of Christendom. Should the Church be more alarmed at the sight of a post-Christian situation in parts of Europe and the Americas than she is in the face of a pre-Christian situation among most of the peoples elsewhere in the world? If this pre-Christian condition of most of mankind today can be regarded with serenity, and even with downright complacency, as a normal phase in the history of salvation, then why should the post-Christian condition of a minority be considered abnormal—almost as a fatal threat to the future life of the whole Church? Perhaps this also is a normal phase in the history of salvation. Or it may be just an inevitable result of the Church's narcissistic introversion, and consequent failure to meet the demands of her prior mission on a scale commensurate with the task and in proportion to her actual ability.

Wherever the Church is turned inward primarily upon its own members, to the neglect of the universal mission, there the Christian reason for the existence of the community has been lost. There the Church signifies nothing more than any other tribal religion; although it may continue on this level to serve its immediate members, providing them with the psychological security, and other helps, that all religions offer. Or it may just die out altogether, having lost its uniquely Christian significance.

Everything on earth, including the historical existence of the Church in this or that particular nation, has not only a beginning in time but also an end. The Christian's land of

[7] *The Church Inside Out*, p. 13.

promise is still in the realm of an eschatological "not yet". The pilgrim people of God will always be visibly somewhere on earth until the end, but not necessarily in this or that particular place where they had once set up their tents. Their presence is primarily symbolical: a sacramental sign. So the growth of the Church into a fully catholic social entity is not the result of a mathematically cumulative process of ever increasing numbers of men among ever increasing numbers of nations. The Church cannot hope to become numerically co-extensive with all nations and all men simultaneously at some future time. "All men and nations" exist only in the consecutiveness of different times and places; so the Church, since she is also subject to this same historical condition, simply cannot expect to become juridically present to "all" at once. All the Councils of the Church, during the first thousand years of Christian history, were held within the boundaries of Turkey.[8] Why is there no discussion today about the urgency of trying to send missionaries to re-build the Church there?

The due priority of missionary work should not be compromised by the fact that things are not perfect among some of the peoples who have already been evangelized once; not even if the Church tends to lose her historical visibility, her relevance and credibility, among those for whom the sign of salvation has already been raised up. The Church does not do sacramentally among the nations more than what Christ has done historically "once and for all". This once-for-all-ness of the Incarnate Word in history belongs to the Church as an historical event among men: an event which, by its temporal presence among a particular people, refers to, and affects significantly,

[8] Cf. "A Changing Church" by J. Blenkinsopp, *The Tablet*, vol. 220, no. 6561 (Feb. 19, 1966), pp. 209 ff.

both the past and the future members of this people.[9]

It is in this way that the last to have been evangelized may become the first, and vice versa; and so it is that the peoples who have not yet known Christ within their own tangible histories have a prior claim on the missionary services of the Church. This is why also the notion of "re-evangelization", invented recently to justify the sending of missionaries to the "de-Christianized masses", is not easily found in Scripture where, indeed, the very opposite notion abounds.

By reason of their immediately distinctive objectives in the service of the Church's total mission, the missionary and the pastoral functions, while they are mutually dependent (one begets the other consecutively among one new people after another), are really different from one another.[10] Now on what grounds could it be maintained that some peoples are more important than others in relation to the universal mission of the Church, and with particular reference to the aims of missionary activity? Priority means precisely this: "before all else". Does the Church need the peoples of one particular area of the world before, or more than, she needs those of other parts? She is the sign to be raised up among the nations, inviting all who have not yet believed.[11] Do the peoples who have not yet been invited need the Church less urgently than those for whom the sign has already been raised up once? Are the seeds of faith to be sown again by

[9] In terms of the biblical notion of "corporate personality", as related to human solidarity in sin and redemption, the present preaching of the Gospel for the first time among a particular people concerns, and significantly embraces, also and at once, both the ancestors and the descendants of this people; for a distinctive ethnic-culture of men unites symbolically the past with the present in reference to the future. Cf. *Catholicism* by Henri de Lubac, s.j. (Burns & Oates, London; Sheed & Ward, New York, 1950), p. 117.

[10] Cf. *Ad Gentes*, no. 6, where, the missionary function is distinguished from the pastoral activity and from "undertakings aimed at the restoration of unity among Christians".

[11] Cf. *Denzinger*, 1794.

missionaries in the same old fields, while never having been sown in so many other fields? Once the seeds have taken root in a field, the missionary must move on to other fields; for the seeds are sown once only by the missionary, and then left until the end under the care of the local husbandman (Matt. 13 : 24-43).

Missionaries, unlike pastors, are not sent to those among whom "Christ has already been named", and for whom the "foundations" of the Church have already been laid (Rom. 15 : 20; I Cor. 3 : 10-15). Nor should they be absorbed in the ordinary service of the existing Christian community (Acts 6 : 2; I Cor. 1 : 17). In order that they who have not been told of him may see (Rom. 15 : 21) the missionary lays the first foundations of the Church among one new people after another, while the indigenous pastor remains to build on the existing foundations. "If his work abides which he has built thereon . . . if his work burns . . ." (I Cor. 3 : 10-15). Meanwhile the missionary has moved on to other fields : to "preach the Gospel in the lands beyond" (II Cor. 10 : 16). Such is the *special* ministry for which some men are "set apart" and "chosen" as missionaries.[12] Repeatedly St Paul had to explain this and to vindicate this specifically missionary vocation, reminding the young churches of the reasons why he could not remain among them or return to them, however much their pastoral problems might have required his services (Gal. 1 : 15-17; 2 : 6-10). He did not return to "re-evangelize" the same peoples again.

Judging from some of Paul's letters to the young churches, and in the light of the subsequent histories of some of these

[12] Cf. *Ad Gentes*, nos. 6, 23, 24, 25, 26, 38, 40, where the "special" and distinctive nature of the missionary vocation is officially recognized, and distinguished from other ministries in the service of the one mission of the Church.

communities, it could perhaps be argued that he should have gone back to them, instead of going on to other peoples. But the Church in history among the nations is an eschatological sign. There is no looking back in missionary activity. The process is eschatological. The end must come some time. The task is progressively brought to "completion" (Rom. 15:18-19) by consecutively "opening the door of faith" (Acts 14:25-27) among one new people after another, so that the preaching of the Gospel "might be completed in the hearing of all nations" (II Tim. 4:17). This witness must *first* be given significantly among all peoples, *and then* shall the end come (Mark 13:10; Matt. 24:14).

The Lord did not suggest that "all" would remain faithful until the end: "When the Son of Man comes, will he find faith on the earth?" (Luke 18:8). Perseverance in the life of public faith is no easy matter even for the Lord's own disciples (Matt 8:26; 28:17). Even after the preaching of the Gospel shall have been completed, the wickedness of men will increase, and charity will grow cold, as nation rises against nation, and pseudo-christs will appeal even to the elect (Matt. 24; Mark 13). "Thus," says Oscar Cullmann, "it is not the case that the coming of the Kingdom depends upon the success of this preaching; it depends rather upon the fact of the preaching."[13]

The Church is not meant to be an everlasting kingdom anywhere on earth among one or another particular people, although churchmen are often enough tempted to particularize the Church in just this way. This is always done at the cost of forgetting, or putting off until "more favourable times", the universal responsibility. The primary task tends to be subordinated to all the "really important" problems of the Church "at home". Even in "mission lands" the major, and sometimes exclusive, concern is usually the care of the

[13] *Christ and Time* by O. Cullmann (SCM Press, London, 1962), p. 160.

existing flock. The remaining unevangelized peoples are generally given the very last consideration. And this is especially true when they happen to be—so like God's originally chosen people—economically destitute, politically insignificant, and culturally "unwashed".[14]

There are, however, some modern mission theorists who suggest that the missionary task of raising up the sign of salvation among the peoples who have not yet believed has already been completed. By equating the biblical "tribes and tongues and peoples and nations" with continents, or countries, or political nations (as distinguished from ethnic-culture units of men), it becomes possible for them to assert that "the Church now exists in almost every nation",[15] and "is now in perceptibly the same situation both in the West and elsewhere."[16] What then remains as the proper concern of missionaries?

In this view, missionary work simply "converges" indistinguishably with all of the other activities by which the Church seeks to "penetrate" some rather vaguely defined "sociological zones" in which "masses" of non-Christians and "de-Christianized" men are found in more or less the same condition all over the world.[17] But one cannot help suspecting that this novel thesis is primarily concerned with "re-evangelization" of the "de-Christianized masses" within certain well-known European and American "sociological zones". The genuine pastoral interest behind this approach

[14] I could provide any number of examples of this situation, from my own first-hand observation in five different African countries.

[15] "The Earthquakes of God" by Eugene L. Smith, in *Christianity A Personal Mission* (World Horizon Reports, no. 30, Maryknoll, N.Y., 1964), p. 36.

[16] "Missions in a New Age," *Herder Correspondence*, vol. 2, no. 6 (June 1965).

[17] Cf. "Missionary Activity: Obstacle or Stimulus to Ecumenism?" by M.-J. Le Guillou, o.p., in *Concilium*, vol. 4, no. 1 (April 1965), pp. 4 ff.

is praiseworthy. But what is also reflected here is the same old inward-turning of missionary zeal for the re-building of Christendom. If everything is missionary work, then nothing is.

Even a superficial acquaintance with current anthropological data, in relation to the presence of Christian communities throughout the world, should suffice to negate the naïve presupposition that the Church exists now among most of the "tribes and tongues and peoples and nations" who constitute contemporary mankind outside of the West. Aside perhaps from the unique coalescence of different peoples during the recent history of North America, we can hardly expect to see the gradual disappearance of most of the world's distinctively diverse ethnic-culture units of men, simply because of their increasing participation in common politico-economic-technocratic structures and social organizations. In spite of such over-all unities in the United Kingdom, for example, the Scots, the Welsh, the English, and the Irish still look upon themselves, and regard each other, as peoples apart (*gentes*) in the human family. On the widely accepted hypothesis of a coming world-civilization, Hans Küng offers this appropriate observation: "Even the merging world-civilization (which in any case will not be Western, Latin, or Roman in character) will not simply eradicate racial, or religious peculiarities, but will in some respects even reinforce them. The closer drawing together of cultural areas promotes the awareness of differences. . . ."[18]

Now what is the present general outlook of the Holy Roman Catholic and Apostolic Church with regard to the world-mission, the universal witness, of Christianity? More than ninety per cent of the Church's visible membership is still found in Europe and the Americas; while less than five

[18] *Structures of the Church* by H. Küng (Burns & Oates, London, 1965), p. 39.

per cent of the Church's total endeavour in the world is actually committed to missionary work among the peoples elsewhere: those who have not yet been evangelized once, and who make up some two thirds of the rapidly increasing world population in areas where the Church has never existed even imperfectly. What has become of the Christian leaven and the ecumenical responsibility of the Church?

It is a remarkable thing about "the Church of the poor" that, in the total perspective of the *oikumene*, there is, comparatively speaking, very little striving after justice and hardly any preaching of the Gospel to the poor. The largest proportion of baptized Christians (those to whom the Church's services are almost entirely directed) live within the West's nineteen richest nations which represent only sixteen per cent of the earth's population and control seventy-five per cent of the world's revenue through a system of economic imperialism.[19] This system, in spite of its paternalistic tokens of "foreign aid", works "for the increasing enrichment of the rich and the increasing impoverishment of the poor", as Yves Congar has pointed out: "an economy based, not on the widest service of the greatest number of men, but on the highest profit of a few."[20] This is not the "poverty" of those who cannot meet the payments due on

[19] Cf. "The Place of Poverty in Christian Life in an Affluent Society" by Yves Congar, o.p., in *Concilium*, vol. 5, no. 2 (May 1966), pp. 28 ff.

[20] *Ibid.*, pp. 34, 35 f.: "The example of the Communist countries shows that the situation can be reversed. . . . It is an established fact that Communism has set up, on the level of whole populations, a social system almost wholly free from the motives of personal profit and the pursuit of money (with the fatal consequence that the poor are maintained in their poverty and even driven further into it). . . . It is in the name of the living God, in the name of the truth of our relationship with him, that we can do no less, though with means very different from those of Communism with its compulsion, to overcome poverty and the profit motive which engenders it. This is the challenge which the present age addresses to Christians. . . ."

a new television set. It is the destitution of those countless millions who must go to bed hungry every night in so many of the "developing countries" of the world. Thirty million of them die each year from malnutrition.[21]

Feeding the hungry, by providing the means to vanquish poverty, ignorance, and disease, is a fundamental Christian responsibility and an integral part of the Christian witness to the whole world. The building of churches is no substitute for this, nor is the preaching of the Word in words only. And what does the giving of superfluities and cast-off clothing have to do with this responsibility? Nothing whatsoever. Perhaps what is needed, in the very first place, is the sound of prophetical voices from the leaders of the Church among the affluent: not the "safe" mouthing of platitudes in defence of the *status quo*. Courage is needed to place this question exactly where it should be: before the conscience of the whole Church, as a matter of salvation or damnation for those who call themselves Christians. In any case, this problem of increasing destitution in the world must become a major concern of the Church as she opens herself to the real *oikumene*. It is now the most immediately practical and pressing aspect of the Church's missionary encounter; for the "developing countries" are more or less co-extensive with her officially designated "mission territories".

---

[21] *Ibid.*, p. 34: "The scandal has existed for a long time, but today it is blatant. It is exposed to the conscience of everybody since, with the modern means of communication, everyone has become present to everyone else. We know the figures of hunger, the statistics of destitution, we have seen the photos of children with their swollen bellies, their hollow eyes, etc. . . . The hungry and the wretched, for their part, have seen the affluence of our buildings, our way of life, our luxuries, our tanks and our guns. . . . Until now, the Christian tradition had not known such a situation, clamouring for a response from the People of God. . . ." For more on this, as *the major problem* facing the Christian conscience today, see the speeches given during Vatican II by A. McCormack, J. J. Norris, and E. E. Swanstrom, *Council Daybook*, Session 3, N.C.W.C., Washington, D.C. (1965), pp. 186 ff., 224 f., 226 f.

It is estimated that, in these areas, hardly more than one thousand priests (out of a world total of about 425,000) are available exclusively or mainly for the service of those who have not yet heard even the name of their Redeemer.[22] The overwhelming majority of missionaries in these same lands are absorbed in the service of the existing Christian communities and young churches. Very many of them are involved full time in educational works which, in many instances, are undertaken primarily as sources of revenue : not primarily as services to the poor who could otherwise receive no education. In general it would be true to say that the least missionary services are available to the most destitute peoples, although there are any number of noble exceptions to this generalization. And, of course, there are countless "justifying" reasons for this over-all situation.

So, to start with, the present missionary resources of the Church are rather parsimonious; and they are so curiously distributed that countless "tribes and tongues and peoples and nations" are completely ignored, costly "prestige buildings are frequently favoured, and many missionaries are forced to function like the members of private clubs. The lavish Apostolic Delegations—palaces for Roman proconsuls —built so recently in some of the "developing countries" are a disconcerting symbol of the Church's "official" approach to the evangelization of the world's poor. "While an enormous mass of people still lack the absolute necessities of life," said the Fathers of Vatican II, "some, even in less advanced countries, live sumptuously or squander wealth."[23]

In fairness, it must be added immediately that not all of the Church's official servants are the same in this matter. Some of them, at least in "mission lands", have no delusions

---

[22] Cf. *Christ to the World*, vol. XI, no. 3, 1966, p. 207.
[23] *Gaudium et Spes*, no. 63.

about their official "dignity", so they do not live in palaces, nor are they chauffeured about in the most expensive vehicles that the offerings of the faithful can buy. Yet there is a scandalously wide, and negatively disturbing, significance to Canon Houtart's angry question: "Were they really sacrilegious hands that wrote 'Blessed are the poor' in tar all over the walls of the villa purchased by the nuncio in Montevideo two years ago?"[24]

If this kind of international vision is going to continue, "*semper idem*", setting the tone of the Church's efforts to become truly catholic among the nations, then what hope is there for a real encounter between the Church of Christ (as distinguished from what Bishop Butler, the former Abbot of Downside, refers to as "an Italian tribal cult"[25]) and the *oikumene*? At this rate the Church in "mission lands" is apt to end up the way it appears to be in Rome: ornate cathedrals turned into museums with a surplus of robed curators whose "full-scale live reproductions of the pageantry of the Renaissance Court"[26] provide one of the unique tourist attractions of the twentieth century.

On top of all this there is an increasing pressure on missionary societies to provide more and more of their dwindling personnel to fill the pastoral gaps in areas where the Church has already been established indigenously, particu-

---

[24] Reported in *The Tablet*, vol. 220, no. 6585 (August 6, 1966), p. 904.

[25] Cf. "Joy in Believing" by B. C. Butler, *The Tablet*, vol. 220, no. 6559 (February 5, 1966), p. 154. In this connection it is worth noting a report that appeared in *Commonweal*, vol. LXXXV, no 12 (Dec. 23, 1966), p. 334; "Of the 47 nuncios and internuncios around the world, 41 are Italian."

[26] John L. McKenzie, s.j., *Authority in The Church* (Geoffrey Chapman, London, Sheed & Ward, New York, 1966), p. 106: "One can understand why our predecessors thought that spiritual authority should be invested with external splendour which symbolized the dignity of authority. We can understand it, even if we think they were wrong in adopting the trappings of secular princes. One should also be able to understand the impatience of modern people with these antiquated trappings."

larly in parts of Latin America.[27] If priority in the distribution of the Church's already meagre missionary resources now must be given to the pastoral care of the existing flock and the re-building of the Church within the cultural sphere of Western Europe, then for the rest of the world there will remain something less than the present "crumbs that fall from the table". And Christianity will continue to be almost exclusively an affair of Europe and the Americas, where "hopefully" a new Christendom may be re-established on the ruins of the old one.

So, without trying to say everything that really ought to be said about the missionary nature of the Church in relation to the real *oikumene*, we have suggested some of the reasons why "it is time the missionary encounter were set firmly at the centre of our theological concern".[28] Only by doing this can we hope to achieve a reintegration of the Church's "varied ministries" which, in so far as they are not explicitly related to the universal mission, tend to become final and very parochial ends in themselves. Liturgical concern, for example, can easily enough degenerate into aesthe-

---

[27] For more on this point, see my article "Mission: The Fundamental Theological Issue", in *Continuum*, vol. 4, no. 1 (Spring 1966), pp. 142 ff.: "The question, first of all, is not whether or not Christians in parts of Latin America should be helped by their brothers to the north. They certainly should be, and very generously too. Rather, the question is this: should those who have been called to the specifically missionary service of the Church be sent to fill the pastoral gaps where the Church has already been established, while the Church has never even existed for most of the peoples elsewhere? In other words, is most of this work, for which missionaries are being sent to Latin America, really the proper and prior object of the Church's missionary activity *as such*? . . . There certainly are other resources, other ministries, that might be drawn upon for the pastoral needs of Latin America. What about all of the priests, for example, who are now tied up in Catholic educational institutions which, in many instances, cater more for those who can afford it than for those who need it." In the United States there is at least one well-known "missionary society" of priests which, through its university commitments, clears an annual profit in millions of dollars.

[28] Van Leeuwen, *op. cit.*, p. 426.

tical purifications. The ecumenical dialogue can be reduced to the level of lofty intellectual amusement. The pastoral service can become therapy for the psychological security of the elect. And religious societies can turn into factories of Pelagian self-perfection, with large departments dedicated to fund-raising.

Only by focusing on God's "ecumenical purpose" can we hope to see a rich and adequate development of the theology of the Christian mission; and only through such a theology will the people of God be able to experience the Pentecostal renewal of their special vocation in relation to the Church's original and final goal. It is by reason of this goal that some men have been chosen to form a representative society, constituted by divine authority, for the sake of all men: "All authority in heaven and on earth has been given to me. Go, *therefore*, make disciples of all nations" (Matt. 28 : 18 f.). Such is the determination, the first and the last orientation, which must characterize all of the Church's activities in the service of her mission to humanity. This Pentecostal determination is at once transcendental, incarnational, and eschatological.

The reorientation of our theological concern must, however, go hand in hand with renewed efforts to get on with the actual task of evangelizing the nations, without any pathological compulsion to keep looking back. Dynamic theology, like that of St Paul, is created in the course of many new missionary journeys and human encounters with those to whom the Church is sent. All of the problems, the challenges, and the risks, must be faced with increased action and reflection together, in faith and singleness of purpose. If the whole Church exists in order to become in historical actuality the sacramental *Lumen Gentium*, then we are all called here and now to work (each according to his position, his gifts, etc.), through whatever inadequate structures are now available, towards this objective.

Once the Church decides to obey this call, by making some concrete commitments that are manifestly related to the real scope of her assignment; and as theologians continue to widen their ecumenical vision, by reflecting on the sights that cannot be seen through the broken panes of a medieval rose window; then the Church's human structures and approaches will be gradually adapted to the demands of the real situation of Christianity's long-awaited missionary encounter with the *oikumene*; and then the liturgists, the ecumenists, the pastors, the religious, etc., will be better able to understand what it is that they are trying to achieve through their own immediately urgent activities. The problem involved in the dialogue with non-Christians, for example, can only be worked out in the course of actual dialogue with them where they live : not in the universities of Europe. There will be no large-scale dialogue unless Christians are actually sent to more of the peoples who have not yet known Christ. And the search for more missionaries will lead right back, not only to the spirit of early Christianity, but to the practice of sending lay-missionaries who were the pioneer evangelists when the Church was originally driven forward by her Pentecostal élan.[29]

What is more urgent than all of this, if "the Church is her true self only when she exists for humanity"? Perhaps one key that may help us towards a fuller opening in this direction was offered by Nietzsche, one of the most provocative of modern Christian prophets, when he said : "My

---

[29] Cf. J. Daniélou, s.j., "Discussion" on "The Priestly Ministry in the Greek Fathers", *The Sacrament of Orders*, p. 128. If our present missionary organizations, structures and approaches could be made more flexible, there would be great scope for lay-missionaries. Without very much more lay participation, and the radical re-structuring that this would entail, it is hard to see how the Church can continue honestly with the claim of being "essentially missionary".

brothers, I do not counsel you to love your neighbour: I counsel you to love him who is furthest from you."[30]

[30] Quoted in *Ethics* by D. Bonhoeffer (Collins, London, Macmillan, New York, 1965), p. 260.

# IX

## Approaching the Others

> The Church will not effectively champion the catholicization of the human race if it cannot itself rise above the provincialism of loving itself more than it does mankind.
>
> LESLIE DEWART

Against the viewpoint presented in the previous pages, is it still possible to hold that the adherents of the multitudinous religions of the world are in good faith only until the Gospel of the kingdom is actually announced to them? This message, as we have noted, reaches relatively fewer men each year. The firm and indigenous establishment of the Church herself among one new people after another is no guarantee that she will remain forever among each of these peoples. So any hope of the coming millennium, chronologically conceived, vanishes progressively into the remote future; and the aim of eventually achieving a homogeneously Christian world population, through the simultaneous existence of the visible Church among all peoples in some vaguely future time, becomes ever more vapid. Such a hope, in any case, would have to be based on the assumption that what is being preached always and everywhere with a Christian label is indeed Christianity: not merely the quasi-Christian folk religion of the preacher.

Even where missionaries may be the instruments of authentic Christianity, there remains the enormous question of communication. Does the message really come through?

Does it penetrate deeply into, and relate integrally with, the seriously experienced concern about human destiny among this or that particular people in the here and now of their own concrete history and limited world-view? To what extent are the terms of communication, used by the ambassadors of Christ, truly intelligible and relevant within the cultural context of those who are waiting to be called "out of every tribe and tongue and people and nation" (Apoc. 5:9)? It is no secret that in some African mission stations Christianity is regarded in practice simply as an item of Western paraphernalia; and it seems thus to be accepted as a sign of "progress", on about the same level with school uniforms, literacy, and hygiene. This question of communicating the message involves the whole complex problem of what anthropologists call the dynamics of culture, with the focus on contact and change.[1]

There is not, and there never has been, a universal culture. From a gross mis-reading of Pierre Teilhard de Chardin, it might be imagined that the ultimate cultural unity of mankind is now developing ostensibly through the world-wide diffusion of Western gadgetry. The religious vision of a people, however, belongs to quite a different level of historical existence. In any event, we ourselves are concerned with, and responsible for, the mission of the Church in relation to the *oikumene* today: not in some hypothetical future.[2] The relentless intrusions of technocracy into the

[1] Cf. *The Church and Cultures*, a mission-oriented manual of anthropology, by Louis J. Luzbetak, Divine Word Publications, Teachny, Illinois, 1963.
[2] Any vision of mankind's future unity arises from an elementary human aspiration which is at least as old as the story of the tower in ancient Babylon. Our reading of the present signs of visible unity, and our evaluation of the currently popular "human unanimization" hypothesis of Teilhard de Chardin, must also take account of the New Testament description of the last days: "when nation will rise up against nation . . . and most men's love will grow cold . . . and all the

once sacrosanct realms of the non-Western cultures is a recent phenomenon. The full implications of this have not yet been clearly discerned.

The secularizing forces of the modern Western world may very well, in the course of time, consign many of the world's religions to the scrap-heap of history, as Professor van Leeuwen has suggested in his persuasive argument that priority should now be given to the development of a Christian theology of secularity—without neglecting all that is required to make the Church truly indigenous whenever and wherever the encounter takes place between the Gospel and the various cultures even as they are now.[3] On the other hand it might also be argued that the technological impact is actually serving to revivify, perhaps by way of reaction, some of the traditional religions; and, while it is certainly

tribes of the earth will mourn . . ." (Matt. 24). There is also the Christian belief that authentic unity is achieved only by love which is made possible only through grace which works for the most part anonymously. In addition to this there are some purely empirical data to be reckoned with : for every sign suggesting a tendency of the modern world towards unity (not uniformity), it might be possible—just by listening to the radio news reports every day—to find several signs suggesting the opposite.

The Teilhardian hypothesis concerning the coming unity of mankind is, moreover, conceived within the terms of an evolutionary process which involves countless wrong-turnings, dead-end movements, and vast wastage in the course of humanity's desired "unanimization". And this hypothesis, which regards man today as "still in an *embryonic state*" of development towards a future social collectivization, is advanced by its author only within the projected historical context of "the hundreds of thousands (probably millions) of years lying ahead of the Mankind we know . . . ". The final outcome of this process is also conditioned by two large assumptions : "that no sidereal accident interferes with the course of events", and that men will "learn to love one another in the very act of drawing together". Cf. Teilhard de Chardin, *The Future of Man*, trans. by N. Denny (Collins, London, 1964), pp. 235, 294 f. See also George H. Tavard, "Tentative Approaches to a Mystique of Unity", in *Journal of Ecumenical Studies*, vol. 3, no. 3 (Fall 1966), p. 512; and Ignace Lepp, *A Christian Philosophy of Existence* (Gill, Dublin, 1965), p. 152.

[3] Van Leeuwen, *op. cit.*, pp. 399 ff.

modifying some of the older cultures, it is also forcing them to reassert themselves in ways that may be either a last ditch stand, or a total renewal. At the present time we simply do not know what the outcome will be. So we must make allowance, as van Leeuwen urges, "for the fact that in principle the twentieth century no longer countenances the isolated community and that therefore one of the most urgent lines of Christian service is to make ready, materially and spiritually, for the arrival of modern civilization."[4]

But the principle remains: the Church must face the peoples of the world, and adapt to them, as they are in the here and now of their own cultural contexts and historical experiences, however static or changing these may be. As things are right now, most men are still seriously concerned with their respective religions; and Christianity is still necessarily embodied in certain historically circumscribed culture-forms, value-systems, and thought patterns. It has become incarnate among some peoples, and through them it is supposed to become incarnate among all the others. If Christianity is still alive, then the missionary encounter with the others is less avoidable than it has ever been before.

The members of a receiving culture, in which Christianity will hopefully be embodied as a result of the Church's mis-

[4] *Ibid.*, p. 424. But generalizations should be avoided in speaking about the advent of this "civilization", as external appearances are apt to be deceiving in many parts of the non-Western world. A closer study of one area after another may reveal that, in spite of political independence and gleaming new cities in the sun, only a fraction of the populations are able to breathe the air of Western secularism, while the socio-economic condition of the masses remains as it has always been, if it is not actually retrogressing. See, for example, René Dumont's *False Start in Africa* (André Deutsch, London, 1966), where John Hatch writes: ". . . In virtually every African state the socio-economic gulf between the peasant masses and the urban *élites* is even greater than the gap between these *élites* and the European and North American norm."

sionary apostolate, are subject to an unconscious screening process whenever alien elements are presented to them. It is notorious that, through such a process of sifting, the more superficial offerings from the outside are the ones most readily accepted, and then frequently given a place of dignity which is out of all proportion with their intrinsic worth. How then is the essence of Christianity to be communicated without all of its irrelevant cultural trappings and historical accretions? Any effort to peel away all of the non-essentials is apt to be a bit too much like peeling an onion in order eventually to arrive at its essence. Perhaps this is a wrong approach altogether. Christianity exists only in the forms of human flesh and mundane history. And communication is not simply a matter of some people giving naked essences, and others just receiving them.

If evangelization is communication, then it should be seen primarily as a matter of mutual giving and receiving. It is a dialogue, leading to a creative symbiosis through acculturation. The peoples of the world need the sign of a servant Saviour who does not quench the wick already burning among them (Isa. 42 : 3; Matt. 5 : 17). And the Church, for the fulfilment of her own catholic nature, needs the cultural "riches of the nations": the "hidden wealth of the peoples" (Isa. 10 : 13-14; 45 : 3, 14; 60 : 4-11). This very thought was expressed by the Fathers of Vatican II, in the following words:

> Truly in the manner of the plan of the Incarnation, the young churches . . . take to themselves in a wonderful exchange all the riches of the nations which were given to Christ as an inheritance (cf. Ps. 2 : 8). These riches are taken from the customs and the traditions of the peoples, from their wisdom and their teachings, their arts and sciences; and all those things are absorbed, which can contribute to proclaiming the

glory of the Creator, to manifesting the grace of the Saviour, and to arranging the Christian life properly.[5]

This is not a new idea. In former times, Christians understood better the practical question of either inventing what is needed, or importing it from elsewhere, or simply using what is found on the spot, in order to ensure the intelligible communication and the authentic incarnation of their message. For Catholic missionaries this question was *theoretically* settled in one of the earliest instructions (in 1695) of the Sacred Congregation for the Propagation of the Faith:

Do not regard it as your task, and do not bring a pressure to bear on the peoples, to change their manners, customs, and uses, unless they are evidently contrary to religion and sound morals. What could be more absurd than to transport France, Spain, Italy, or some other European country to China? Do not introduce all that to them, but only the faith, which does not despise or destroy the manners and customs of any people, always supposing that they are not evil, but rather wishes to see them preserved unharmed. It is the nature of men to love and treasure above everything else their own country and that which belongs to it; in consequence there is no stronger cause for alienation and hate than an attack on local customs, especially when these go back to venerable antiquity.

[5] *Ad Gentes*, no. 22: ". . . There will be a clearer appreciation of the ways that faith can seek for understanding by using the philosophy and wisdom of these peoples, and of how their customs, outlook on life, and social systems, can be harmonized with the manner of living taught by divine revelation. Thus the way will be opened for a more profound adaptation covering every aspect of the Christian life. By such a procedure, every appearance of syncretism and false particularism can be excluded, and the Christian life will be accommodated to the mentality and characteristics of each culture; and the particular traditions of the families of the nations, together with their own proper endowments, illumined by the light of the Gospel, will be absorbed in a catholic unity. And finally, the new individual churches, adorned with their own traditions, will have their own place in the ecclesiastical communion. . . ."

This is more especially the case, when an attempt is made to introduce the customs of another people in place of those which have been abolished. . . .[6]

Are not the traditional religious expressions of men among the greatest and the most immemorial of their cultural riches? Can such venerable "manners, customs and uses" be shoved aside with impunity?

Indeed, the Church has already, as a matter of necessity, borrowed extensively from non-Christians and from their religions. "It would be quite childish to assume," as Paul Simon has clearly pointed out, "that the apostles had invented, on rational lines, new forms of liturgical life. . . . They were no more able to invent cultural and religious forms than to invent a new language. This applies to everything connected with religious worship and sermons, whether language, formal acts, or outward arrangements."[7] In the articulation of their new faith the early Christians did not draw merely from the religious heritage of their Jewish Lord and Master. They strove also to translate their message positively into the contemporary Gentile world. From an abundance of evidence, we know that this process of assimilation went on for centuries.

Even from the proscribed "paganism", which Symmachus had defended to no immediately apparent avail, the

---

[6] *Collect. Prop. Fide.*, 1907, vol. I, p. 42; the translation here is taken from *A History of Christian Missions* by Stephen Neill (Penguin Books, Harmondsworth, 1964), p. 179.

[7] *The Human Element in the Church of Christ* by Paul Simon (Newman, Westminster, 1954), p. 31; cf. also Paul Tillich, *Theology of Culture*, pp. 42, 47, 48, 49: "In abbreviation: religion is the substance of culture, culture is the form of religion. . . . Every religious act, not only in organized religion, but also in the most intimate movement of the soul, is culturally formed. . . . Religious language is ordinary language, changed under the power of what it expresses. . . ." So Christianity can speak to the different peoples of the world only through *their* respective cultural forms, religious structures, and languages, none of which are in themselves holy, universal, and unalterable.

Church has absorbed and transformed a multitude of theological concepts and religious forms. Some of Saint Paul's terms and phrases seem to have come directly from the mystery religions which were common in the Roman Empire of his time, while others were obviously borrowed by him from the writings of the Stoics. Saint Ambrose himself made a bold effort to combine elements of Stoicism with Christianity in a synthesis which, through its influence on monasticism in the Middle Ages, has left an indelible mark on Christian morality and ascetical practice. The Christian cult of the saints, and early iconography, reflect the gradual movement away from the common polytheism of the times. Some Church officials even encouraged the practice whereby the veneration of the apostles, martyrs and angels became a thinly veiled substitute for the worship of local gods; and some of the representations of Christ were not without traces leading unmistakably to Apollo or to Orpheus. The nuptial rite of the Church in the ninth century, as prescribed by Pope Nicholas I, was precisely that of the "pagan" Romans, with the Mass in place of the customary sacrifice.

Professor Latourette, in his monumental study of the Church's historical growth, provides many more examples, with their appropriate references,[8] of this accommodating attitude which was expressed so well in Pope Gregory the Great's famous instruction to missionaries working among the "barbarians" of Britain:

> Since the people are accustomed, when they assemble for sacrifice, to kill many oxen in sacrifice to the devils, it seems reasonable to appoint a festival for the people by way of exchange. The people must learn to slay their cattle not in honour of the devil, but in honour of God and for their

[8] *A History of the Expansion of Christianity* by Kenneth Scott Latourette (Harper, New York, 1937), vol. I, pp. 298 ff.

own food; when they have eaten and are full, then they must render thanks to the giver of all good things. If we allow them to use outward joys, they are more likely to find their way to the true inner joy. . . . It is doubtless impossible to cut off all abuses at once from rough hearts, just as the man who sets out to climb a high mountain does not advance by leaps and bounds, but goes upward step by step and pace by pace.[9]

But, it must be asked, what about the religious wealth of the peoples living outside of Europe?

Some of the Jesuit missionaries of the seventeenth and eighteenth centuries certainly tried hard and courageously to keep the Church moving faithfully, according to her own original inspiration, in the direction of an ever-widening cultural ecumenism. The continuation of their dialogue with the cultures of China and India, along the radically incarnational lines initiated by Matthew Ricci and Robert de Nobili, might well have transformed the whole subsequent history of the world. But the effort was foiled by the provincialism of the Church's European princes and proconsuls. And this failure, in the opinion of Arnold Toynbee, "is going to loom out in retrospect as one of the epoch-making events of our modern Western history when this local history is seen in its true light as an incident in the general history of mankind".[10]

The full story of this disaster is long and complex. It involves some shamefully bitter rivalries among the missionaries themselves, intensively nationalistic feelings among Christian brothers, some of the Church's dubious political commitments, theological and cultural obtuseness on a massive scale, and some incredible arrogance in high

[9] *Patr. Lat.*, 77, 1215, 1187; the translation here is taken from Neill, *op. sit.*, p. 68.
[10] *Civilization on Trial* by Arnold Toynbee (Oxford University Press, London, 1946), p. 85.

places. At one stage, towards the end of the lengthy controversy, nine Italian Cardinals in Rome decided that the Emperor of China had not properly understood the meaning of certain key words in the Chinese language; and their lofty decision had a fatal impact in each of the subsequent stages of the debate.

The enlightened dialogue, both in China and in India, was finally and irrevocably cut off, in the mid-eighteenth century, by the Roman keepers of Europe's religion. The formal termination of the whole affair is credited to Pope Benedict XIV, who is noted in Church history manuals for having "promoted good feelings towards the Holy See among the various European rulers",[11] and for having cultivated a personal friendship with Voltaire who described Benedict as "the glory of Rome and the father of the world".[12] Since his time, and up until the recent Council, the practices of the Church in Italy have been generally regarded as normative for the rest of the world.

Nevertheless, an impressive amount of lip service has since been given to the missionary ideal of adaptation or accommodation. To deny this ideal, at least in theory, would amount to denying the nature of the Church who seems somehow able to survive for long periods while, in practice, contradicting the highest demands of her own nature. The principle of adaptation, as formulated officially and repeatedly by the Church's servants in Rome, flows directly from the earth-shaking revelation that God Himself did not think it imprudent, nor any loss to His dignity, to empty Himself (cf. Phil. 2 : 7-8), by taking on the flesh and the whole culture of one particularly intractable and "underdeveloped" tribe of human beings.

[11] Cf. *An Outline of Church History* by Joseph McSorley (B. Herder, St. Louis, 1949), p. 737.
[12] *Ibid.*, p. 738.

Inflexible ecclesiastical structures, related more to the Church's past political experiences in Europe than to her ever present evangelical world-mission, have promoted among missionaries an almost pathological attitude of literal conformity, and a stifling fear of innovation. Prudence has come to mean simply doing what was done the last time. But much more than this is behind the Europeanizing policy of Christian missionaries, Protestants as well as Catholics, during the past two hundred years or so. They have been working zealously, and many of them continue to do so today, under an immense cloud of cultural pride and spiritual arrogance: the "monstrously anti-humanist and presumptuous theory", as Leopold Sedar Senghor sees it, that European civilization is the universal civilization, "to be imposed, unmodified, on all peoples and continents. . . ."[13] As Tom Mboya put it, more concretely:

In the early mission days the Church objected to the African dances as primitive and uncivilized, and for years there was complete conflict between the Church and those Africans who wanted to continue African traditions and customs and stood for African culture. The Church came almost to preach to us in terms of a blueprint of the British social and cultural system, which they regarded as representing civilization and Christianity. To us this confusing of the European way of life with Christianity was entirely a contradiction of terms.[14]

This surely is the basic reason for whatever failures may be justly attributed to the missionary effort of the Church in our time. Missionaries have generally by-passed the cul-

[13] From an address, "What is Negritude?" given by Senghor at Oxford University, October 1961; partial quotations found in *The Other Dialogue* by Joseph Gremillion (Doubleday, Garden City, 1965), p. 253.

[14] *Freedom and After* by Tom Mboya (André Deutsch, London, 1963), p. 20; also, for similar thoughts expressed thirty years ago by an angry young anthropologist who has since become the President of his country: *Facing Mount Kenya* by Jomo Kenyatta (Secker & Warburg, London, 1938), pp. 269, 271.

tures of the peoples to whom they have been sent: no creative dialogue, no significant adaptation, no incarnational encounter.

And this might as well be said also, since it is widely recognized already (although not officially it seems): Even the local clergy of the young churches in Africa—many, if not most of them—fall into President Julius Nyerere's descriptive category of "Black Europeans": those who have come to believe, as a result of their education, that "we had no indigenous culture of our own, or that what we had was so uncouth as to be a cause of shame to us, and not a cause of pride."[15] So it is that the young Christian communities of Africa still have today the appearance of a European spiritual colony. Africans are still being given unpronounceable European names at baptism, while the rare practice of using authentic African names is generally regarded as "verging on near heresy", or at least "a dangerous innovation".

At long last some efforts are now being made, although still on a modest scale, to use genuine African music in the Christian churches of this rhythmic land whose peoples have already contributed so much to the music of the rest of the world. But it has not yet been widely noticed by the servants of the Church that a man is more deeply moved by his own traditional art forms than by anything foreign; even if his own may be, as Mwalimu Nyerere has noted, "nothing more than the shaking of pebbles in a tin".[16] And how much, even more so, does this apply to indigenous forms of prayer and of worship? The universal mission of the Church, and her real dignity, are still gravely compromised by a widespread failure to recognize the necessity of accommodation through dialogue, in obedience to the

[15] Cf. *President's Address to the National Assembly* by Julius Nyerere, 10 December, 1962, Dar es Salaam.
[16] *Ibid.*, p. 21.

Church's own frequently articulated principle of adaptation.[17]

However, there has been in recent years a wide, if sometimes rude, awakening. Professor Bolaji Idowu of the University of Ibadan has offered a penetrating and responsible criticism of the Christian missionary effort in Nigeria. The reflections contained in his slim volume, *Towards an Indigenous Church*,[18] apply with equal validity to the situation in East Africa, and doubtless to many other areas as well. Among others, Canon David Paton has also given us some hard thoughts to ponder along these same lines in his *Christian Missions and the Judgment of God*.[19] And Roland Allen, an unheeded prophet, wrote on this subject in 1912, telling us almost everything that we are just now beginning to realize in this last hour of the Christian missions as we have known them.[20]

Some of the more revolutionary aspects of this re-thinking of the Church's incarnational-ecumenical purpose were suggested by Raymond Panikkar, when he wrote that "Christ did not come to found religion, and much less a new religion, but to fulfil all justice (Matt. 3:15) and to bring to its fullness every religion of the world (Matt. 5:17; Heb. 1:1 ff.)."[21] We have seen in this chapter some indications of the Church's practice, *in the past*, of assimilating the religious

[17] Once again, in the words of *Ad Gentes*, no. 10, this recurring theme of Vatican II: "The Church must embody herself among all these groups in the same positive way that Christ, by His Incarnation, bound Himself to the definite social and cultural conditions of the men with whom He conversed."

[18] Oxford University Press, London, Ibadan, 1965.

[19] SCM Press, London, 1953; cf. also Paton's contribution in *The Missionary Church in East and West*.

[20] Cf. Roland Allen, *Missionary Methods: St. Paul's or Ours?* (World Dominion Press, London, 1960); *The Spontaneous Expansion of the Church* (World Dominion Press, London, 1960); and *The Ministry of the Spirit: Selected Writings of Roland Allen*, ed. by D. M. Paton (World Dominion Press, London, 1965).

[21] R. Panikkar, in *Christian Revelation and World Religions*, p. 168.

forms and expressions of the cultures in which she has become incarnate. Now what of the *future*? Panikkar continues:

> Christianity is, sociologically speaking, certainly one religion; it is the ancient paganism, or, to be more precise, the complex Hebrew-Hellenic-Graeco-Latin-Celtic-Gothic-modern religion *converted* to Christ with more or less success. Christianity in India . . . should not be an imported, fully-fledged and highly developed religion, but Hinduism itself *converted* —or Islam, or Buddhism, or whatever it may be.

> It has to be immediately added that this converted Hinduism is, substantially, the same as the old one and yet different, a new creation (II Cor. 5:17).[22]

Just how far can we go with this principle of adaptation? Perhaps it is also time now to give some thought to the long-standing negative attitude of Christians with regard to the social institution of polygamy. Even slave owners in former times were permitted to enter into the life of the Church without first having to dispose of their highly questionable socio-economic possessions. But polygamists are still being told that, before responding to the call of explicit Christian faith, which is also directed to them, they must first violate the just contracts previously made in good faith by themselves with other persons. Is this matter of polygamy beyond question in a Church that for centuries took a very tolerant attitude towards the socio-economic institution of slavery which everyone today—the opinions of Augustine and Aquinas notwithstanding—would consider utterly incompatible with Christianity?

In some societies the whole family and socio-economic

---

[22] *Ibid.*, p. 169; for more on this see also *The Unknown Christ of Hinduism* by R. Panikkar (Darton, Longman & Todd, 1964); and "The Church and Non-Christian Religions" by Piet Schoonenberg, s.j., in *The Meaning of the Church*, ed. D. Flanagan (Gill, Dublin, 1966).

structure is intimately bound up with the immemorial practice of polygamy which, even according to the traditional
Christian ethics, is not in itself evil, since it was clearly
permitted by God under the old covenant. Does the New
Testament contain any explicit prohibition against this
custom, aside from that referring to the qualities required
of an official servant of the Church: that he should be a
man of only one wife (I Tim. 3:2, 12; Titus 1:6)?

Such practices as adultery, fornication, prostitution, and
homosexuality were singled out for repudiation in the New
Testament; but nowhere is monogamy explicitly com-
manded and polygamy forbidden.[23] As the prevailing custom of the Greco-Roman world at that time, monogamy
was simply taken as the normal and obvious point of departure; and for centuries thereafter the prevailing secular or
tribal norms of marriage were accepted as Christian practice. The biblical norms of marriage, and the cultural
practices associated with this secular reality among the
various peoples of Europe were largely determined by the
prevailing view of the position of women in this or that
particular society; and only gradually did marriage become
an ecclesiastical and liturgical affair.[24]

Even the medieval theological developments through
which marriage was recognized as one of the "seven important sacraments", symbolically representing the relationship between Christ and His Church, would not seem to be
essentially incompatible with polygamy: for the Church is
plural. Is it possible that the traditional Christian insistence
on monogamy is just another result of the Western ethnocentrism of theologians and churchmen who have never

[23] Cf. *Marriage: Secular Reality and Saving Mystery*, vol. I, by E.
Schillebeeckx (Sheed and Ward, London, 1965), p. 284.

[24] *Ibid.*, vol. II, pp. 3 ff., 201 ff., 212 ff.; for more on this question see
Eugene Hillman, c.s.sp., "Polygyny Reconsidered", in *Concilium*, vol.
3, no. 4 (1968).

really considered seriously what the practices of Christianity might be like had the Church become extensively indigenous, and had the New Testament been interpreted by theologians of various non-Western cultural backgrounds?

If the Church today seriously intends once again to "effectively champion the catholicization of the human race", and thus to "rise above the provincialism of loving itself more than it does mankind",[25] then this question of polygamy is just one of the very many problems that will have to be faced in the near future.[26] And this will have to be done in the same bold way that the Church once faced such questions as the necessity of maintaining Jewish religio-cultural practices among the Gentiles who were turning to the Lord. The Judaizers have long since been replaced by Europeanizers. But the *oikumene* remains; and it is still, for the most part, untouched by Christianity.

[25] Leslie Dewart, "Peace and the Papal Witness", *Continuum*, vol. 4, no. 1 (Spring 1966), p. 129.

[26] Perhaps the most immediately urgent of these problems on the practical level is the much needed reform of the Church's official ministry in relation to the wider ecumenical mission of Christianity. On this, see Roland Allen, *The Ministry of the Spirit*, pp. 139-46.

# Index of Names